Golf Basics

the short game

Golf Basics

the short game

Derek Lawrenson

TRIUMPH
BOOKS
CHICAGO

First published in Great Britain in 1996
by Hamlyn an imprint of Reed Consumer Books Limited
Michelin House, 81 Fulham Road, London SW3 6RB
and Auckland, Melbourne, Singapore and Toronto

ISBN 1-57243-120-2

Published in the United States by
Triumph Books
644 South Clark Street, Chicago, Illinois 60605
Tel (312) 939 3330 Fax (312) 663 3557

Produced by Mandarin Offset
Printed and bound in Hong Kong

Special photography: Nick Walker
Book design: Birgit Eggers
Cover design: Salvatore Concialdi
Art director: Keith Martin
Picture research: Jenny Faithful

Acknowledgements
It would not have been possible to write this book without the expert knowledge
of Scott Cranfield, who is rapidly gaining a reputation as one of the brightest
young teaching professionals in the game.

    How good is Scott? Well the publisher of this book, Rab MacWilliam, has
cadged three lessons and is already hitting the ball straight. And if you'd
seen how he was hitting the ball before you'd know what a considerable
achievement that is. Rab is looking forward to continued improvement upon
studying this book.

    In addition to Rab, from Hamlyn I'd also like to thank sports editor Adam
Ward, who remained an irrepressible source of good humour despite the three-
pronged assault of photographic shoots, my words, and watching West Ham
every week.

Editor's note
Many thanks to Robert Walker and Chris for their help during the photographic shoot.

Photographic Acknowledgements
Allsport /Simon Bruty 102 bottom, /David Cannon 86 right; Golf Monthly 68
bottom, /Nick Walker 12, 13 left, 13 right, 73, 75, 92, 93, 94, 95 right, 97 left,
107; Hamlyn /Action Plus 58, 72, 82, 100 centre, 100 top, /Nick Walker 9 centre,
9 left, 9 right, 10 left, 10 right, 11 bottom left, 11 bottom right, 11 top, 15 top
left, 15 top right, 15 bottom left, 15 bottom right, 16 bottom left, 16 top right, 17
right, 17 left, 19 bottom, 20, 21 left, 21 right, 21 centre, 26 bottom, 26 top, 27
right, 27 left, 28 right, 28 left, 29, 30 bottom, 30 top left, 30 top right, 31, 32 /3,
33 left, 33 right, 33 centre, 34 right, 34 centre, 34 left, 35, 36, 37 right, 37 left,
38, 39 left, 39 right, 40, 41 left, 41 right, 42 inset, 42 main, 43 left, 43 right, 44
right, 44 left, 45 left, 45 right, 46, 47, 48, 49 right, 49 left, 51 top right, 51 bottom left, 51 top left, 51 bottom right, 52, 53, 54 right, 54 left, 55, 62, 64 /65 top,
65 right, 65 centre, 65, 66 bottom, 66 centre, 66 top, 67 centre, 67 top, 67 bottom, 68 top, 69 left, 69 right, 70 /71, 74, 75 bottom left, 75 bottom right, 76, 77
below, 77 above, 79, 80 right, 80 left, 81, 83 left, 85, 95 left, 99 top, 99 bottom,
108; Ben Hogan UK 23; Popperfoto /Bob Thomas Sports 90 bottom left; Reed
International Books Ltd 70 /71; Phil Sheldon back jacket flap, 7 bottom, 7 top,
8, 19 top, 24 bottom, 24 top, 56, 57, 59, 60 top right, 60 top left, 63, 70, 78, 83
right, 86 left, 89 top, 90 top right, 90 bottom right, 90 top left, 96 right, 96 left,
97 right, 100 bottom, 102 top, 103, 104 top, 105, /Sidney Harris 89 bottom, /Jan
Traylen 60 bottom, 84, 104 bottom; Roger Tidman 106 top, 106 left

Many thanks to the following companies for supplying equipment for the
photographic shoot: Titleist (golf balls, golf clubs, shoes and gloves) and
Oscar Jacobson (clothing).

Scott Cranfield uses Gary Player clubs and wears Reebok shoes.

Introduction

Golf is one of the few major sports that is not prejudiced against the fat person or the thin, the tall or the small, the young or the old. While it offers enc-ouragement to the fitness fanatic, remember that Craig Stadler, nicknamed 'The Walrus' with good reason, once won The US Masters.

That is why it appeals to people across all walks of life. It can be thrilling, exhilarating, frustrating, maddening, indeed just about any adjective you care to mention. But what makes it so special, is that it can be any, or all, of these things to anyone.

Hyatt Hotels once did a survey which showed that more business deals were conducted on the golf course than in the boardroom. But other courses are full of people who have never done a business deal in their lives but who just enjoy the game's simple pleasures. Golf is also one of the few major sports that doesn't harbour, or encourage, cheating.

There is no referee, no umpire. You are the sole judge of your actions. Golf is the easiest game at which to cheat and that is why few people ever do it, and why being caught cheating is the worst thing that can happen to a golfer. A solicitor who was caught regularly moving his ball was not only thrown out of his local club, but his business went to pot as well. His clients clearly thought that if he could cheat at golf then he must be cheating in his professional life as well.

It is fair to say that the game has an intimidating air about it. Go down to your local private club and invariably there will be a sign at the front gate stressing the 'private' bit. The sport's rules appear forbidding and convoluted. Even the great Nick Faldo twice fell foul of the rules in 1994. And how long do you need to be playing to score respectably? How long before that complicated grip starts to feel comfortable? Will I ever stop slicing the ball? What the hell does cavity blade mean? Golf is the game that launches a thousand questions.

It is also fair to say that the sport has an expensive air to it. Golf clubs can be pricey instruments. Furthermore, if you ever pluck up the courage to get past the front entrance you may find that your local private club will cost you several thousand pounds to join. If, that is, you can get in at all.

But golf doesn't have to be any of these things. This book sets out to demystify some of the game's language and its codes. The instruction section is easy to read and easy to follow. I've attempted to explain things with humour as well – something not usually associated with golf instruction books. Many leave the reader confused and baffled and ready to take up something less taxing like running a marathon. Others prefer the pompous language route, whereby the 'expert' tries to impress the student with his knowledge and command of golfing terms. Do yourself a favour and forget those routes.

Leap over the first few hurdles and you'll find equipment that won't cost you a fortune. You'll discover a club that is a bastion of warmth and hospitality. You'll know what to do when your ball is buried in a bunker or lies at the bottom of a lake, and instead of fearing for your life when you hear you're playing in a tournament with a shotgun start, you'll have the time of your life.

The American sportswriter Grantland Rice got it right in 1920 when he wrote: 'Golf is about twenty per cent mechanics and technique. The other eighty per cent is philosophy, humour, tragedy, romance, melodrama, companionship, camaraderie, cussedness and conversation.' These books are designed to give you the first twenty per cent; they'll also help on those days when the golfing shot you can't play is sapping your morale faster than a raging toothache.

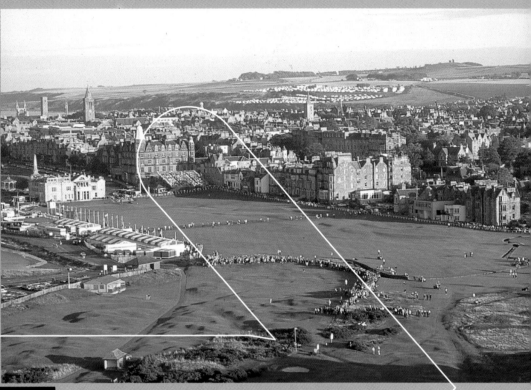

Above: St Andrews in Fife, Scotland, is known as the home of golf and certainly the setting is incomparable. Over the years it has played host to 25 Open Championships.

Left: Is that a scowl we see on Nick Faldo's face? Always remember that not even the best golfers can hit good shots all the time.

'There are three ways of learning golf: by study,
which is the most wearisome; by imitation,
which is the most fallacious; and by experience,
which is the most bitter.'

Robert Browning in *A History of Golf,* 1955

THE BASIC SWING

Develop your own swing

Eamonn Darcy prepares to launch his
drive on the 18th at St Andrews. The
pristine building in the background is the
clubhouse of the Royal and Ancient Golf
Club of St Andrews.

In recent years the game of golf has become obsessed by instruction. On television, a tournament leader's swing is broken down into segments and each analysed for faults. It's as if there is only way to swing a club. There isn't.

Some of the great golfers had swings that made orthodox players weep and which defied supposedly golden rules. Gary Player couldn't swing the club without knocking himself over – so much for perfect balance. Arnold Palmer attacked the ball as if it was threatening his life – so much for smooth rhythm. In his prime, Jack Nicklaus committed a cardinal sin – his right elbow refused to remain tucked against his side at the top of the backswing. The great achievements of these three, arguably the greatest trio of golfers in the last 40 years, should convince you that there is room for an individualist swing. If you're still not convinced, just go and have a look at Eamonn Darcy.

That genial Irishman is a case in point. For years he carried on doing his own thing, won £1 million, a bag of tournaments, and was a Ryder Cup hero. He was feted wherever he went. Then he tried to change one of golf's strangest swings into something more fashionable. He fell off the chart for a couple of years. The message is clear: if something is working for you for heaven's sake don't go and change it because a magazine article tells you it is incorrect. Just go out and enjoy your golf and to hell with worrying whether it looks right or not.

What is important to grasp, though, is that there are fundamentals that, if implemented in your swing, will make you a more consistent golfer. If you are a raw recruit, then you are perfect material for the pages that follow – you haven't got into any bad habits that need to be swept away!

The most important thing in golf is to possess a sound basic swing and set-up. The best way of achieving this is to absorb the advice given in this book by top teaching professional Scott

Cranfield (below) and then follow up by taking a course of lessons from a respected local pro. Remember: you don't have to be a member of a club to have lessons. If such expense is outside your

budget then try group lessons. Many pay-as-you-play courses, offer such packages and a lot of people prefer to be taught alongside five or six other players and find it less intimidating.

Lessons and videos

The first thing to do after reading this book – and its companion volume of course! – is to book yourself half a dozen lessons with a local professional who has a good reputation for teaching. The Professional Golfers' Association did a survey a couple of years ago where they asked golfers what was the number one source for getting tips and advice on how to play. The overwhelming answer was their friends, with books like this one and magazines second and professionals an extremely poor third.

Friends, books, and magazines can only take you so far. There can be no substitute for first-hand commentary from an expert. Most will give you a discount if you book a block of six lessons. If that is still outside your budget, then some of the larger golfing establishments do group lessons. Of course this is not as helpful as one-to-one sessions, but I'm prepared to bet that you'll learn far more than from your 16 handicap playing partner.

If you're a total beginner and a little apprehensive about going for a one-to-one with your local pro, then these group lessons may help you initially. The professional will video your swing and talk you through it. The more you learn, the more you will be able to trawl through some of the rubbish that is written on the subject these days and pick out the nuggets.

One thing to remember: golf is perhaps the hardest of all sports to learn to play. In the early days, it is very easy to get discouraged as you duff the ball about 10 yards off the tee and find a long iron an impossible club to use. Just persevere. Don't book yourself a tee-time at St Andrews three months from the day that you first pick up a club. Improvement in golf comes in fractions.

 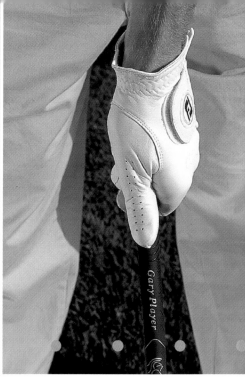

'Never give up. Give up on golf and you give up on life. If you give up that first time, it's easier to give up the second, third, and fourth times.'

Tom Watson

The Grip

Dear Reader, it is at this point, as you try to enact the following manoeuvres, that we are about to have a little falling out. There is no point trying to make light of the following: gripping a golf club for the first time is about as comfortable an experience as the first time you get behind the wheel.

All that I can offer in consolation is that once you've stopped throwing this book around the room in frustration and have got used to it, a solid grip will save you endless hours of irritation in the future.

Just don't try to cheat. Don't think you can get away with holding the golf club any old way: you can't. And if you think it's awkward now, then it's nothing compared to trying later to cure an incorrect grip.

How hard should you be gripping a golf club? This is a matter of some debate. Sam Snead, the great American pro and perhaps the greatest swinger of a golf club of all time, would tell his pupils to imagine they were holding a little dove in their hands. Most modern-day teachers, however, recommend you grip it a little harder than that.

Basically, you've got some leeway here. Just don't grip it so hard that it's as if the club is a dangling rope to which you're attached and if you let go you plunge into a vast ravine. And don't go to the other extreme and grip it so softly, you're imitating a wimpish handshake.

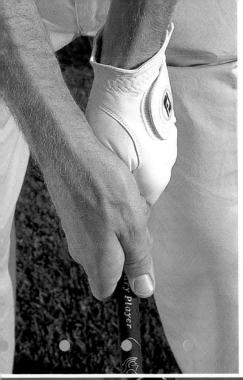

For a right-handed golfer, the first step is to place the club in the left hand, gripping it just below the top of the club so that it runs between the crook of the first finger, and along the 'pads' of the rest of your fingers.

Now close your fingers around the club, so that your thumb is pointing directly down the shaft. The top of the club should be visible above your hand.

Your right hand, which can be linked to your left in one of two principal ways (see below) should conceal your left thumb and form a perfect 'V' between right thumb and forefinger down the centre of the shaft.

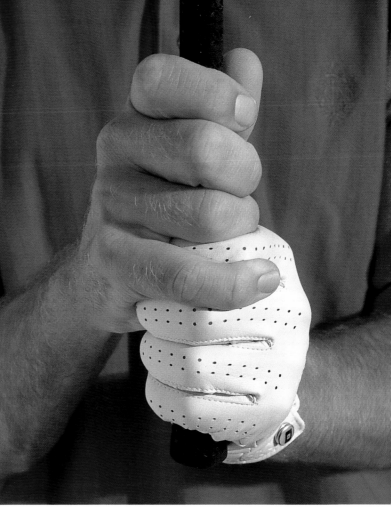

The interlocking grip is widely used and gives you the feeling that you have a secure hold on your club. The forefinger of the left hand is positioned on the grip of the club between the third and small fingers of your right hand.

The most popular grip simply involves placing the small finger of your right hand over the fold between the first and second fingers of your left and closing your fingers around the club. It is known as the overlapping grip.

Many players are unsure as to how far they should stand from the ball but there is one easy way to solve this dilemma. First, stand up straight and hold the club out in front of you, as above...

Stance

Golf may be a sport where you walk miles, but it is, in fact, played in inches and when everything is out of synch by inches, it can have a disastrous effect. That is why it is the hardest game to master. For example: position the ball in front of your right toe and you will hook the ball horrendously. Now bring it back three inches so that it is opposite your left heel, swing exactly the same and, aha!, straight as a dye it flies.

The stance is the easy bit. Stand with your feet parallel and shoulder width apart. Your right foot should be pointed slightly outwards. Your knees should be flexed a little. Stand up – don't crouch. For the wooden club shots, the ball should be positioned opposite your left heel, and for the irons, an inch or two further back. If you placed an iron club on the floor in front of your feet now, the club should be pointing exactly at the target.

How far should you stand from the ball? The hands should be away from the body, particularly with the long clubs, but the important thing is to feel comfortable and relaxed. Tension in the arm or leg muscles causes more bad shots than perhaps anything else.

Here's an easy tip to remember if you're not sure how far away to stand: grip the club and hold it out in front of you with your arms slightly flexed. Now bring it slowly down to the ground. When you reach the ground, that is how far you should stand from the ball.

'You have to build up the pupil's belief that you
are delighted to see that they are nowhere near
as absolutely hopeless as they think they are.'

Teaching pro Billy Burke

...then flex the knees (as above), adopting
the proper stance, with your feet shoulder
width apart...

...now, bend naturally from the waist.
When the club has reached the ground
you will have discovered how far you
should be standing from the ball.

'You make twenty mistakes in
your backswing and correct
half of them with your follow-
through but unfortunately you
haven't quite balanced the
budget.'

Teaching pro Harry Ortiz to a pupil

1. The perfect address position for a mid-iron. The ball is positioned centre-left in the stance.

2. Halfway back and the left elbow has remained straight but not rigid. The right elbow remains nicely tucked against the right side.

Backswing

The other day I was reading a book on the golf swing and the section on the backswing seemed to go on longer than *War and Peace*. At the end of it, the teacher offered seven checkpoints for the pupil to remember during the backswing. Seven! If anyone can remember seven checkpoints about anything during the second or so it takes to complete the backswing then he should apply to be Head of MENSA.

Here's a couple of good tips: keep your left elbow straight throughout, though not so rigid that it causes tension, and keep your right elbow tucked in adjacent to the side of your body. This will feel awkward at first, but try to remember these two things as you swing the club loosely back and forth. Try to get a feel for the rhythm of the swing and to teach your muscles what is required.

On the backswing, your upper body will be rotating and your lower body will be resisting. Your eyes should not leave the ball. If all has gone well your shoulders will have turned 90 degrees and your hips half that amount. Your left knee will automatically be pointing towards the ball. If you are fit and agile, the club should be horizontal and pointing directly towards the target. If you're not, then take the club back as far as feels comfortable. Be patient with the backswing. It is an unnatural manoeuvre, but absolutely vital because the follow-through is a breeze if the backswing is properly completed. Good luck!

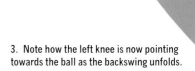

3. Note how the left knee is now pointing towards the ball as the backswing unfolds.

4. The top of the backswing: the club is now pointing towards the target; the left knee is over the ball; the left elbow is still straight; the left shoulder is over the ball. The shoulders have turned through 90 degrees and the hips half that amount.

1 3
2 4

'Six years are needed to make a golfer –
three years to learn the game, then another
three to unlearn all you have learned in
the first three years. You might be a golfer
when you arrive at this stage, but more
likely you're just starting.'

Walter Hagen

FROM LEFT TO RIGHT

The legs have initiated the follow-through. Note how the right knee is no longer pointing over the ball.

Here the swing is uncoiling nicely towards the hitting area. The legs are driving through, but not so fast that they cause the loss of control of the club.

Note the difference in the wrists between this picture and the last one. They have 'rolled over' during the hitting of the ball, with impact coming at the halfway point. Note also the way the eyes remain focussed on the ground.

The finish: now the head has come up naturally; the body facing the target; perfect balance has been maintained.

The hitting area and follow-through

If the backswing is when you coil both your body and the club and imagine all sorts of exciting possibilities, then the follow-through is when you uncoil and realise all your potential. That's the theory anyway. Having got the backswing right, don't spoil it all by coming down from the top like a hurricane entering Miami Beach. Keep that left arm nicely straight. Maintain your rhythm. Keep your eye on the ball. Let it all unfold naturally. It all sounds so easy doesn't it? Here's a couple of other things to digest. Make sure your body turns throughout and doesn't tilt. This is one of the most common faults in golf. It is caused because the player is so anxious to give the ball a helping hand that he leans back as he begins the follow-through. The result is disastrous. Just practise that turning sensation in your living room (alright, upstairs if you don't want your partner to laugh at you). Feel your upper body turning to the right during the backswing and then back towards the centre during the first part of the follow-through, then your whole body turning towards the left during the second part. You should be perfectly balanced at the end, with your right toe pointing towards the ground. Grasp all that and the ball will go 200 yards. But be prepared for a few hiccups along the way. Golf is like that. Just remember two things:

1. Never get so discouraged that you feel like chucking it in.

2. Never get so encouraged that you think you've got it licked.

the sho

It seems perverse that, if a 400 yard par four is played correctly, a player will take only two shots to cover 394 yards and then two more to cover the last six. Even when played less accurately for a five, it's odds-on that a player will take two shots to cover 390 yards and three to cover the final ten.

In this book we'll concentrate on all the shots that come in the last few yards. If your driving and long iron play make you want to stick out your chest and feel smug, then the time to get serious and really save yourself a lot of strokes, is with the short irons. This is where you make or break your score, as the first paragraph indicates. After all, it doesn't matter how much you improve, unless you are a gorilla you'll never be able to cover 394 yards in anything better than two strokes; however, confidence in your chipping and putting will help you turn three shots into two and even two into one.

We will analyse all shots from 150 yards in to help you improve. In particular we'll concentrate on the shots that cause acute problems to most beginners: the bunker shot from a compacted lie; the pitch shot from a bare lie; the flop shot over a bunker on to a sloping green. Yes, I know, just thinking of these shots is enough to send shivers down your spine, but we'll help soothe your doubts and fears.

Here we come on to the key factor regarding the short game: confidence. You'll have often heard it said that golf, like many major sports, is mostly played in the mind. The short game is 90% played in the head. It is primarily about confidence. But to have confidence you must have the correct technique to play each shot and then you have to practice that technique until it becomes second nature. The great thing about practising your short game is you don't need acres of land in which to do it. You can practise your chipping in your back garden. You can practice your putting stroke on the carpet at home.

rt game

Therefore don't worry about not having the time. Ten minutes every other evening just chipping a few balls in your garden will make an enormous difference when you come to play your golf out on the course.

Of course practising a pitch shot over water is a little difficult, unless you've got an Ascot home like Nick Faldo with a stream running through a three-tier garden. But it's surprising, once you've grasped the principles regarding the short chips and pitches how the fears you had regarding those of 40 yards or so also fall away.

Putting is a game in itself – the game within a game – and it doesn't matter how good you become, or how confident you feel as you go out on to the course, you will still have days when you couldn't hole a putt if your life depended on it. So I'm afraid the bad news is that those days never completely disappear, no matter how good you become.

This book, though, will show you how to ensure that you enjoy some good days with your putter as well – days when God is clearly in his heaven, when you feel like the Chosen One and that you can't do a thing wrong on the greens.

Putting is the great equaliser: it's the one area of the game where all players, be they professionals or humble amateurs, look much the same. This is where you can see the importance of confidence: if a professional holes a 10ft putt to break an unlucky streak, you can almost guarantee that they'll hole another shortly after. Something has slotted into place and whatever the something is, it invariably comes back to confidence.

But confidence is much easier to talk about than to acquire: it is borne of good technique and long hours of perseverance. This book will show you how to acquire the technique. It will also demonstrate that perseverance doesn't have to be one of the most boring words in the English language.

Top: Gary Player practised so hard out of bunkers at times that his hands started to bleed. The reward was a well-deserved reputation as the finest golfer of all time out of sand.

Bottom: Many golfers are intimidated by the prospect of a 100 yard wedge shot that involves a carry over water, with the green tucked in close behind.

THE CLUBS

ONE MINUTE TIP

Always remember that you can save many more shots practising your short game than with your long irons or driver. If your practice time is limited and you don't know whether to work on your ball striking with your woods or your technique around the greens, plump for the latter.

After all, think of a player like Bernard Gallacher, who not only captained three Ryder Cup teams, but also competed in eight. This was a man who was fairly unimpressive off the tee, but more than made up for it with tenacity and confidence around the greens. There's no way that he would have achieved all he did in the game if his skills had been the other way round, where he had been great off the tee, but possessed an average short game.

Seven iron to wedge

The short irons comprise those clubs from the seven iron down through to the wedge. The higher the club number, the shorter the shot and the greater the need for accuracy. Any reasonably proficient player will be hoping to hit the green at least eight times out of ten with a club numbered seven, eight or nine. Any professional will be truly disgusted if he doesn't get the ball within 20ft of the pin with a wedge.

Most beginners start out hitting shots with clubs such as the seven iron and quickly make friends with them – they are straightforward to use. The natural loft of the club means there is no problem getting the ball airborne. The accent is on finesse and accuracy, rather than power, and the vast majority of players feel comfortable trying to transmit these qualities with a golf club.

The maximum distance we are talking about here is 150 yards, about the outer limit that a good player will expect to hit a seven iron. More typically, the average amateur will hit it between 130–140 yards, and because it is so important that you hit the greens frequently with these clubs, it is vital you know just how far you hit your seven iron. It is a simple thing to discover. Go to the nearest patch of land and pace off 150 yards from your bag, placing an umbrella in the ground. Now hit 20 seven iron shots to the umbrella and note the range between your best and worst.

If most of the balls have gathered in a cluster or gone about the same distance, then clearly that is how far you can hit a seven iron. But don't fall into the web that traps so many players: one of the 20 balls has reached the umbrella and so the next time the player has a 150 yard shot to a green he takes a seven iron, thrashes it to death, and wonders why he hits it badly, finishing 15 yards short. Sheer folly! Once you know your capabilities with a seven iron, take ten yards off for each club of a higher denomination.

FROM LEFT TO RIGHT

For all shots played with short irons, adopt your normal address position with the ball centre-left in your stance.

Control is the name of the game here rather than length and so for a 100 yard shot the backswing need not be so full as one where the ball needs to go further.

Rhythm is the other key factor. Swing smoothly. And don't be tempted to look up too soon to see where the ball has gone!

As the follow-through is completed so the body turns and the head comes up naturally. The result is a smooth shot over the water rather than a thinned one into it.

Wedges

At one time, every self-respecting professional would carry four woods in his bag. Then John Daly decided, if it was all the same to everybody, that he'd prefer four wedges. People laughed at him. Daly, with one wood in his bag, then won the USPGA Championship without the benefit of a practice round. People laughed no more.

Current conventional wisdom suggests that two wedges will get the job done. A pitching wedge will allow you to play not only the shots that the name suggests, but also little chips from around the green. With a sand wedge you can obviously play bunker shots, and also 'flop' shots where you need to land the ball softly on the putting surface.

So why would you need any more? Isn't three or four the, um, thin end of the wedge? According to Barry Willet, Mizuno's club maker on the European Tour, it has something to do with the design of modern courses. 'It is something that has happened in the last four years. Before, the pros would probably have had a standard wedge at 50 degrees and a sand-iron at 56.'

'Then they started getting into more bunkers around greens so now they like their sand-iron between 56 and 58 degrees (modern bunkers tend to be wider and longer and so the player requires the extra loft for more height to enable the ball to land softly). If their standard wedge is set at 50 that gives them quite a big gap, so they tend to carry a wedge in between set at 54 and, in Daly's case, a lobber wedge at 60.'

A third wedge is useful for the amateur who would rather hit a full shot as often as possible. Clearly, a 60 degree wedge enables you to hit a 60-yard shot with a full swing, rather than a half-shot with a normal wedge, or a three-quarter one with a sand wedge.

Jamie Spence makes this point: 'I get more use out of an extra sand wedge than I would out of a two iron because it gives me many more options. At a lot of new courses like East Sussex National, where the greens are fast and there is a lot of rough around them, you get a lot of different lies and you need three wedges.'

So there is the argument in favour. I tend to think that a newcomer to the sport would get more confused by, rather than benefit from, three wedges. You may also want to bear in mind Ian Woosnam's thoughts on the matter. 'Why do I only carry two wedges when a lot of other players carry three? Simple. They need to. You only need three wedges if you can't play the shots. Look at Severiano Ballesteros, the short game master. Does he use three wedges? No. That answers the question doesn't it?'

QUICK FACT

In 1932 Gene Sarazen came up with the perfect solution for his weakness out of bunkers – he invented the sand wedge. He knew the reason for his poor play was that the niblick (wedge) wasn't designed to get underneath the ball, taking a layer of sand, so he put a flange on the back of it. 'I spent hours practising that shot and getting the flange just right and it got so I would bet even money I could get down in two out of sand,' Sarazen recalled, years later. In 1935 he became the first player to win all four major championships at least once, a feat that only three players – Ben Hogan, Jack Nicklaus, and Gary Player – have since emulated.

Players now have an unrivalled choice of wedges with which to play shots around the greens. The higher the loft the more spin the player will get and the further the ball will travel in the air at the expense of distance.

Over the years Bernhard Langer has
suffered more than any other modern
player on the greens. Consequently he
has been a man of many styles, a man of
many putters.

Few people have come closer to
mastering the black art of putting
than Ben Crenshaw. Here, the Texan
celebrates another holed putt.

Putting - the black art

It is perhaps the greatest paradox in sport that something that anyone can play
and enjoy without any tuition should also be the one thing that destroys
careers because people have failed to master it.

No-one epitomised the impossible black art of putting more than Sam Snead,
whom many consider the finest swinger of a golf club of all time, yet who was
reduced to putting 'croquet' style because of his problems on the greens.

Bernhard Langer is the most famous sufferer in recent years. Three times he
has been inflicted with the acute golfing condition known as the 'yips', and we
deal in detail with this debilitating yet fascinating ailment later in this book.
But isn't it truly amazing that men who can conquer the mysterious dynamics
of the golf swing with seemingly effortless ease are left blubbering wrecks by
the easiest stroke of all? Surely there is nothing too difficult in trying to propel
a ball 1.68 inches in diameter into a hole that is more than twice the size?

Ah, but this is the black art, remember. When an American company devised
a putting machine and carried out tests in perfect and constant conditions,
they were amazed to find that it could not hole every putt. The machine was in
perfect working order; the human element had been taken away – it was all
down to simple geometry and physics. And still it missed.

The leading practitioners of the black art are blessed indeed, and their
putters have become almost as famous as themselves. Ben Crenshaw's putter
is known as 'Little Ben', and when it went missing for a time, the American was
distraught. Since it was returned he has never let it out of his sight. If he
goes on an aeroplane, he takes it on board with him. When checking in at a
tournament his clubs are left in storage, but the putter goes back with him to
the hotel room.

A person who putts well can often be quite a source of grievance to other
golfers, particularly in match play competitions – it's as if they are using some
sort of unfair method to win. Ben Hogan, a poor putter, once growled at Billy
Casper, who wasn't: 'If you couldn't putt, you'd be selling hot-dogs outside
the ropes.'

It isn't just the most intense players who suffer either. Mark James, as philo-
sophical as they come, was reduced last year to using a broomhandle putter.

It's plausible to conclude that good putters are born that way, blessed with
a natural sense of feel, hand-to-eye co-ordination, and confidence. Yet even
that isn't the whole tale: good putters can easily lose their talent. Look at Tom
Watson, from 1975-1985 one of the great putters that the game has seen, and
one of the worst from 1985-1995.

The final proof that putting is a black art comes on those occasions, which
have happened to all of us, when we stand over a putt and just know that we are
about to hole it. What mysterious force is at play here? What is happening to
allow us to see the line as clear as day and know that the putt is going to drop?
And why does it never last and why, three or four putts later, is everything
about as clear as mud again?

QUICK FACT

It was at the 1967 Ryder Cup that
one golf writer, who is best left
nameless, was approached in the
exhibition tent by an odd-looking
little man with a goatee beard
who was rattling on about a putter
he had invented. He insisted that
the writer have two and try them
out. The writer did. He couldn't
get on with them. He gave them
away. Years later he was rather
sorry he hadn't kept them. Two
of the first Ping putters off the
production line – for that is what
they were, and the man with the
goatee beard was the inventor
Karsten Solheim – would be worth
rather a lot of money today.

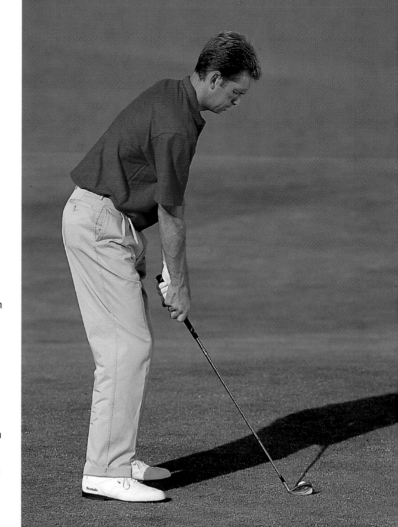

FROM LEFT TO RIGHT

Because the shafts are shorter, you will be standing closer to the ball when playing the short irons and you will feel as if you are slightly more crouched from the waist up.

Control is everything with the short irons. The shorter shafts promote a greater degree of control, leaving the player to concentrate on completing a smooth swing.

Short game shots often result in a small divot being taken, as seen far right. This is because the loft of the club cuts into the turf at impact, promoting spin. Just remember to replace the turf afterwards!

ONE MINUTE TIP

When practising your shorter irons, make sure that you have a target at which to aim. These are the clubs, of course, that you will invariably be using to locate the greens and so you need to be deadly accurate. Try sticking an umbrella into the ground and aim to get within 30ft of it at least 75% of the time.

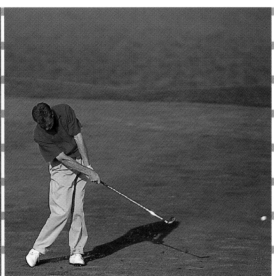

Seven to nine irons - technique

When using either a seven, eight, or nine iron, there is no change in general technique from that used for the longer clubs. The shafts are shorter than with the long irons and so the knee bend should be a little more pronounced and the forearms more relaxed. The ball should be positioned in your stance halfway between the middle of your feet and your left toe.

Because the shafts are shorter, you will be standing closer to the ball and with less freedom to turn the shoulders, your backswing will inevitably not be as long as it would be with your driver. This is a good thing as the key with these shots is control and accuracy. Clearly if your backswing is slightly shorter, then that offers more control, and more control means more accuracy.

You often hear of professionals hitting a 'hard' seven iron, but if you think a shot calls for everything you've got with an eight iron, then opt for smoothness and rhythm and hit a seven. It's impossible to over-stress that the key with short irons is that distance doesn't get you any brownie points. Off the tee an extra 20 yards might set up an easier second shot, but, with a short iron, it's getting the ball close to the pin that counts. You are much more likely to achieve that with a smooth eight rather than a hard seven. This is one area where adopting the ideas of the top pros can harm to your own game. Because a player is standing closer to the ball, owing to the shorter shaft, it is usually not long before a player gains confidence with these clubs. A few crisp short iron shots out of the middle of the club and everyone starts to get the golfing bug.

This page, left: When a tree stands between your ball and the green the smart thing to do is to use the loft provided by a short iron to play over the top of it.

This page, right: When stymied by a tree, take a short iron to relocate the fairway. Position the ball opposite your back foot so you don't hit behind it.

Opposite page: Don't be a hero. When faced with a tree completely inhibiting your follow-through, simply take a penalty drop. The potential for injury, not to mention the expense of a broken club, far outweighs the spurious benefit.

ONE MINUTE TIP

On shorter par threes, you'll occasionally be hitting anything from a seven iron to a wedge; something to be avoided is to tee up the ball at the normal height. For these shots, many good players will dispense with a tee altogether on the grounds that they will get more feel without one. But if you feel more comfortable with a tee, make sure it is firmly stuck in the ground with the ball nestling just the merest smidgen off the turf.

When to use and how far to hit

As we have already stated, the vast majority of full seven to nine iron shots will be used to fire to greens. However, these clubs are also good trouble-shooters. Occasionally you'll find yourself having to hit a nine iron over trees to relocate your fairway or a punched seven iron out of woodland as you try to get back on to the mown stuff, but hopefully not too often!

The seven iron, however, can play a greater part in the decision-making process. Say you're playing a par five that you can reach with a driver, three iron, and a wedge. Now you don't like hitting a three iron and you're worried that it will leave you in trouble. In that case consider hitting a driver and then two seven irons. The most important thing in golf is to get the job done and if it is a little unorthodox then so be it.

From the moment you consider your game good enough to step out regularly on to a golf course, you need to know how far you hit your short irons. Earlier in this book I suggested a simple tip to help you find out (see page 21). The alternative is to learn the hard way: to find yourself with a 135 yard shot over water; to say to yourself that it looks like a nine iron; and then strike it beautifully, watch it adoringly, expecting it to nestle next to the flag and see it instead go splash. Anyone who has been through this experience quickly learns how far he can hit each club.

Far left: Don't be too ambitious when playing from heavy rough. Relocating the fairway is paramount. A bogey is never disastrous but don't squander two shots trying for an extra 20 yards.

Left: If the lie is particularly bad, as in this instance, breaking the wrists early means the clubhead will descend to the back of the ball at a steeper angle, thus cutting down the amount of rough that gets between club and ball.

Bottom left: Grass stains in the middle of the club face are the classic result of a shot played from a flying lie. Felt great didn't it? Well, until your ball finished 20 yards through the back of the green.

Right: A classic flying lie. The ball is on a tuft of grass and there's no way of meeting the back of the ball without hitting the grass first. The result is a loss of spin and more distance: so take a club less than normal.

Divot, heavy rough and flying lie

The short irons have adequate loft to deal with heavy rough, and the rougher it is, the shorter iron you will need. Clearly if you are up to your neck in it, you may have to consider taking an unplayable lie, but the general rule is that if you can see it, or any part of it, then a sand wedge will be able to get the ball out.

What is most important when playing from heavy rough is to keep your eye on the ball. The temptation is to lift the head early in order to witness your miraculous recovery shot. However, there will be no miraculous recovery shot if you do. Playing from heavy rough is one instance when you can swing harder than normal, but not if it is at the expense of rhythm. You still have to have complete control of the clubhead as there is always the danger that the ball will not budge, or not budge enough for you to relocate the fairway.

A flying lie occurs when a ball finishes in the first cut of rough, with a cushion of grass underneath it. That grass comes between the clubface and the ball and ends any chance a player has of imparting spin, so the ball ends up flying much further than normal.

You'll soon be able to deduce whether you have a flying lie or not. The ball feels extremely sweet off the clubface but clearly, if it is flying 20 yards more or so, the final result might not be so sweet. But once you've detected a flying lie, you can make allowances and avoid over-running your target by taking a club less than you would normally choose.

QUICK FACT

One of the great seven iron shots from trouble of all time came on the final hole of the 1988 US Masters at Augusta. Sandy Lyle, needing a par to tie Mark Calcavecchia, found the fairway bunker on the left with his tee shot. He had 151 yards to go, but needed to get the ball up quickly as the bunker has a steep face. He chose a seven iron and hit the perfect shot – the ball finished 8ft from the hole. Never mind a par: he made the putt for a birdie to win by one, becoming the first British player to win the event.

PITCHING

ONE MINUTE TIP

This is one shot when your head must remain still until after you've made contact with the ball. Nick Faldo has adopted the practice of not taking his eye off where the ball lay until his club has reached the horizontal on the follow-through. If you're prone to looking up before you've made contact with the ball this is one tip for you to try.

Note how perfectly still the head is in the last photograph. The result is a clean hit, and the ball airborne and bound for the green.

General technique

The short game is primarily about confidence, but if your technique is incorrect then confidence will always elude you. There are four shots you need to master around the greens and if you can achieve a degree of solidity with each of them, then you are well on your way to lowering your handicap dramatically. The four are: the pitch, the chip, the bunker shot, the putt. The pitch covers various shots from 100 yards from the flag, but generally what we are talking about here is the lobbed shot landing the ball softly on the green. The object is to get height on the ball and impart backspin. The pleasing thing from your point of view is that, equipped with the sand wedge, you have just the club for the task.

The basic pitch shot requires a half swing: you take the club back to the horizontal and then through to the same position. Place the ball in the centre of your stance with your weight on the left side. Your stance should be slightly open, with your shoulders pointing to the left of the target as you view it. Your hands should be ahead of the ball. It is here, before even starting the shot, that most beginners fall down. They want to put most of their weight on the right side and their hands behind the ball in order to scoop the ball into the air. The results are always disastrous – as I said, the sand wedge is equipped to do all the work.

Having got the right address position, you're more than halfway on the road to completing your task. Simply swing the club to the horizontal in the normal way and then back through the ball.

Don't try to help it into the air, and don't quit on the shot – swing normally and smoothly. A modicum of practice and this becomes one of the easiest, but one of the most vital, shots in any golfer's repertoire. In every round there will be at least one or two occasions when a pitch shot is called for. Approach it with dread and you'll need three or four or even more shots to complete the hole; but approach with confidence, and you will start to fancy your chances of getting down in two. Once you reach that happy state of affairs, you'll really start to enjoy your golf.

For this shot the ball should be positioned in the middle of the feet. The backswing should be three-quarters in length.

In the follow-through the emphasis should be on rhythm. Practise enough and you will become confident in your ability to produce a smooth swing.

The ball is now on its way but the head remains still, waiting for the turn of the body towards the target to bring the ball into vision.

The full pitch

With 80 yards left to go to the green, you have plenty of options: a canny low shot with a nine iron; a half shot with a pitching wedge; or a full blown pitch with a sand wedge.

If there is water in front of the green or a hazard, then the last is your best option – unless you're playing into a strong breeze, in which case go with the wedge and hit a three-quarters shot.

There is no need to adopt any strange techniques with a full pitch shot. Just swing as you would with the wedge. Again, because the shaft is the shortest in your bag, you will not be able to complete the backswing.

Adopt your normal stance for a short iron shot. Once more, the key things are rhythm and control. Make sure you accelerate through the ball and aim for a crisp, sure contact. The sand wedge is one club you should not force under any circumstances, but when playing to a pin cut tight behind a bunker or to a small green, it is a most useful weapon.

QUICK FACT

Corey Pavin is one of the best short iron players around and he favours hitting full shots as often as he can. When Pavin was at the peak of his powers in 1993, he could actually visualise himself holing pitch shots from 80 yards away. Which just goes to show what confidence can do for you!

Pitching over a bunker

Pitching over a bunker is 10% technique and 90% confidence. There are two pitfalls that always trap the unwary beginner:

1. They're so worried about the shot that they 'quit' on it, decelerating into the hitting area. The result is that they hit behind the ball and it trickles into the very bunker they're trying to avoid, or, even more humiliatingly, stops short – therefore they've got the same shot to play over again.

2. They're so worried about the shot that they're looking to see where it has finished, even before they've completed the backswing. The result is that they thin it and the ball flies past the target at great speed, invariably leaving the player in a similar predicament over the other side of the green.

Clearly the key that links both these pitching shots is the fear of botching it up. The bunker is no longer just a hazard but a snarling menace, with an insatiable desire for your golf ball. Another common failing is the worry that the club does not possess enough loft to get the ball over the sand, so the player tries to scoop it over. Nothing will more certainly lead to failure.

First things first: make sure your technique is correct. The ball should be set in the middle of your stance; the weight should slightly favour the left-hand side. The most important aspects now are control and rhythm. The best way to

ONE MINUTE TIP

Think half 'n' half: half a backswing and half a follow-through. The swing should involve a slight acceleration through the ball but not so much that it disturbs your rhythm. That is all important. If you're ever at a professional tournament, just wander over to the practice ground and watch as the professionals work on this shot. One thing will be quickly apparent: their half-swings all possess the same tempo and all are as smooth as silk.

This is one of those shots that is a bread and butter stroke for a professional yet scares the life out of high handicappers. The ball is positioned in the middle of the feet and the stance slightly open, i.e. pointing to the left of the flag.

Note the early wrist break and the half-backswing. The steeper angle of attack promotes both spin and loft which are the two essentials of this shot.

Keep the legs 'quiet'; it is a hands and arms shot where the object is to keep the clubhead moving through the area of impact.

ensure the former is with a backswing restricted to half your normal length –
any more than that and you're asking for trouble. The follow-through will
almost certainly be about the same length if you have mastered the rhythm.
Swing normally. Think smooth and keep your legs still. Let the club do the work
– it will have more than enough loft to get the ball over the bunker.

Once you have mastered these techniques, the next step is to conquer your
mind. If you are sure of your technique then the bunker reverts to its role of
being just another hazard. Now the shot is all about confidence and feel.
Practise it enough and both come automatically. In time you'll be able to play
this shot not just with a sand wedge, but also with a wedge and a nine iron as
well, depending on the height of the bunker.

Being an accomplished exponent of this pitching shot is guaranteed to save
you strokes every round. It also stops you falling victim to one of the most
destructive elements in the sport. There's nothing worse than covering a 400-
yard hole in two and then marking down a six because you've needed two
pitch shots. There's no hidden mystery as to why you felt you played well and
yet you struggled to break three figures. If you can't pitch, you can't score. It's
as simple as that.

Bermuda rough

For those of us brought up on a staple diet of the chip and run shot, playing in America is often a humiliating experience. There you will find that many courses have been seeded with Bermuda grass around the greens. Bermuda grass is tough and feisty and when your ball lands in a two-inch crop, it doesn't sit up as in Britain but plunges downwards. This is why you find many Americans chip with a wedge or a sand wedge. Bermuda greens are lightning fast and so the object is to play a shot that has the properties of a chip which will roll upon landing, but to play it like a pitch so that it flops gently onto the green.

If you are playing a course with Bermuda grass for the first time, you will be happy if you can keep any chip on the green. When European golfers first try their hand on the US tour, they always struggle and this is invariably because they are learning to cope with the peculiarities of this pitch-cum-chip shot.

Bermuda rough: dontcha just hate it? The ball sits down and the recovery shot owes more than a touch to luck.

QUICK FACT

In the 1982 US Open at Pebble Beach in California, Tom Watson was tied with Jack Nicklaus when he hooked his three iron tee shot to the 17th into the Bermuda rough by the green. With the pin 10ft away, many commentators were already preparing to salute another major victory for the Golden Bear. Watson thought otherwise: 'I'm going to hole this,' he told his caddie. The caddie thought he'd be lucky to get it within 20ft. But Watson popped the ball out onto the edge of the green, and it ran down hitting the pin with a firm rap before disappearing below ground. Watson birdied the last hole as well to confirm a memorable victory.

More and more courses are now using grasses which cause the ball to sit down in the rough around the greens. I think this Americanisation of British courses is a great shame, but if you play at such a course or travel abroad a fair deal, then it's something with which you need to come to terms.

Adopt your normal pitching stance, keeping the hands well ahead of the ball. The object is to hit the ball with a downward blow so that it pops out of the rough. Keep the rhythm smooth and keep accelerating through the ball – any deceleration and the Bermuda grass will wrap itself around the clubface and the ball will move about two inches – if you're lucky. It's a shot that requires a fair bit of patience and practice. If the only time you encounter Bermuda rough is on your golfing holiday every other year, don't worry about it and don't let it spoil your round!

The feet are close together for this shot. Again an exaggerated wrist-break is used to hit the back of the ball without the clubhead becoming tangled up in the Bermuda.

Confidence is the key. It is absolutely vital that you don't quit at impact on this shot, or the ball will go nowhere and you'll end up playing another shot from the rough.

The ball will sit down more than usual if it is in a divot, so don't even think about lifting your head to look at the result until well after impact.

Divot

With luck, you'll never have to face playing a pitch shot from a divot. Certainly it is something that the members of the Oxfordshire, a course that is always in perfect condition, rarely have to worry about. But sometimes you'll play a course where there is a hole that leaves a player a 40-yard pitch shot over water and here you might find a gathering of divots and your ball may well finish in one.

Yes, by all means, take a couple of seconds to curse your luck, but this is really another shot which looks worse than it is. Once more, adopt your normal stance for a pitch shot: the ball in the middle of your feet; your weight predominantly on your left side; your shoulders and feet slightly open to the target.

Your object here is for the club to meet the back of the ball just before taking a smidgen of turf and the best way for you to do this is with a controlled half-backswing, leading to a smooth acceleration through the ball. Once you've successfully completed this shot, you'll be surprised how much of the fear has evaporated the next time.

Bare lie

A pitch shot from a bare lie is much more common. Even on the best links courses, the ground around the bunkers near the greens can get very parched. Many amateurs dread playing a pitch shot over a bunker from a bare lie. The professionals would much rather have it than a cushioned lie because it enables them to impart spin on the ball. Once again this is a shot where basic technique will help you overcome any fears – the normal pitch shot rules apply.

Once again the feet are close together for this shot. Play it with any wedge other than a sand wedge; the flange at the bottom of the sand wedge will cause you to hit the ground before the ball and the club will 'bounce' into the ball.

Note the perfect weight distribution. Weight must be distributed equally between the left and right feet – too much toward the right and you will scoop the ball into the air; too much to the left and you will strike the top of the ball.

ONE MINUTE TIP

If there are two common faults among the poor pitchers of this world, it is that they have their weight on the right-hand side in a misguided attempt to scoop the ball into the air, their backswing is too long and they therefore decelerate through the ball. Concentrate on these two things and the days of poor pitching will soon belong to your previous life.

The shank

There are two words that should be avoided in golfing company and this is one of them. The other is the 'yips', a degenerative putting disease that has finished the greatest of golfers. But the shank is the shot that all average players fear the most because it is the most destructive shot in the game to affect them.

It occurs when the face of the blade is open at impact and the club has been swung on an incorrect path line, the ball comes off the hosel instead of the club face and squirts away at right angles to the target.

The worst thing about the shank is how quickly it can become a habit; once it has happened, it can rapidly infect the mind and if things reach that stage, then standing over a pitch shot becomes very fearful.

The first corrective stage is in the set-up; make sure the ball is in the middle of your stance; that your weight is on your left side; the shoulders and feet are slightly open to the target; and the ball is positioned in the middle of your club face when you set the club down and not opposite the hosel. Now the back-swing: take the club back to the horizontal, resisting any temptation to roll the wrists early; feel that you're in control on the downswing, that you have retained your rhythm, and that you're not decelerating as you come towards the ball.

Left (main pic): One of the ugliest shots you can hit. A shank usually occurs when the club is swung on an incorrect flight path and instead of the club face it is the hosel that strikes the ball.

Left (inset): The result is terribly destructive. The ball flies at right angles to the intended target and invariably into deep trouble.

Right: Note where the ball is positioned on the club face. Often a shank is caused simply through the ball being positioned opposite the hosel at address.

Far right: That's better! A smooth and rythmical swing, its flight path from in to out, and the ball is now heading in the intended direction.

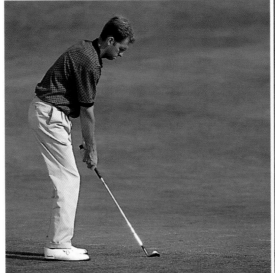 

ONE MINUTE TIP

Correcting the odd shank is not a difficult thing and you may find you'll go for years before you suffer another. But if it is commonplace in your game, then your muscles have been trained to work in a certain, incorrect way and you've got problems. Explaining the way out of this problem in a book is one thing but you may want to seek professional advice to teach you where the club should be and so retrain your muscles.

The flop shot

No, this isn't the description given to a make or break shot that you mess up. The flop shot is a highly-skilled pitch, where the player imparts so much back-spin on the ball that it ascends almost vertically before stopping on a sixpence.

For all his reputation as a long-hitter, John Daly is also one of the masters of this delicate shot. I once saw him play the second hole in the Open at Muirfield and, having almost driven the green at this shortish par four, he had left himself the following shot: a pitch from a bare lie over a bunker, with the pin cut 10ft from the sand.

I thought he would have to play for the safe half of the green and settle for a four. I couldn't see any other option. Daly could – he took out his 60 degree wedge, almost completed a full backswing and to a stunned audience hit the ball very hard. It was propelled vertically, must have risen 30ft in the air, landing just over the bunker before finishing next to the hole. Phil Mickelson, another of the young Americans brought up on these lofted wedges, once

ONE MINUTE TIP

For heaven's sake don't try this shot for the first time when playing on the golf course. For players like Mickelson and Daly, it took years of practice and, if you don't pull it off, you could find that your acceleration through the ball has propelled it into some-body's back garden. The flop shot is a useful weapon to have – but there are plenty of others that need to be given higher priority.

completed the following shot in a college event: trying to play short of a ditch in front of the green, he miscalculated to the extent that the ball rolled down towards the ditch, but came to rest on the downslope. He couldn't see how he could get the ball up quickly enough from this downward lie to clear the ditch, so he turned the other way. The spectators thought he was just chipping the ball back on to the fairway from whence he came; but Mickelson thrashed at the ball with all his might and it stayed on the clubface so long that it went back over his head, over the ditch, and on to the front of the green. How to play that shot only Mickelson knows, just as only Daly knows how he got that tap-in birdie at Muirfield, but playing a variation of the flop shot is within the grasp of most players.

Adopt your normal pitching stance with the blade slightly open (you need a slightly fuller swing than usual) and accelerate through the ball – it is the club-head speed that imparts the backspin and gets the ball up quickly.

FROM LEFT TO RIGHT

This is the 60 degree wedge shot – the one the pros love to show off. The normal address position, except for a slightly exaggerated bend at the knees.

The wrist break is early and the swing a full one. The object is to hit the ball at such a steep angle that it leaves the ground almost vertically.

Now the fun bit! Get it wrong at impact and the ball will be on the other side of that lake in the background.

Get it right, however, and it is one of the most satisfying shots in golf. The ball lands as if possessing a parachute and nestles adjacent to the flag.

1. Learn to visualise the shot:

   Before you actually try to play the pitch shot
   you've left yourself, it is important to make a
   mental note of what you're trying to achieve,
   something you can learn on the practice ground.
   Try playing to a practice green and visualise
   each time the shot you're trying to execute:
   picture where the ball is going to land on the
   green and aim for that spot.

Before playing a pitch shot it is a
good idea to stand behind the
ball and get a mental picture of
what you are trying to achieve.

2. Get into the same mental routine whenever you're confronted with a pitch shot.
   Commit the following check list to memory:

a) Have I visualised the shot I want to play?

b) Is the ball in the middle of my stance, with my feet no more than 15 inches apart?

c) Is most of my weight on my left hand side, thus promoting a crisp contact with
   the ball?

d) Are my shoulders open and therefore pointing to the left of the target?

e) Finally: half a backswing and half a follow-through.

3. If you've lost confidence completely with your pitching, then separate each of the fundamentals and practise them in turn. First practise the half swing with out a ball at your feet. Let your muscles feel what you're actually asking of them. Now practise with your weight on your left hand side and feel the bottom of the club just touching the ground at what would be the point of impact. Now try it with a ball in front of you. Keep the same smooth rhythm and build up your confidence.

Clearly the aim is to get the ball as close to the hole as possible so make sure you are properly aligned to the target.

4. The mistake that many people make when they are practising pitch shots is to do so from a perfect lie each time and then they're puzzled as to why they make a mess of a shot from a difficult lie when they're out on the course. Try practising a few pitch shots from the rough, and also from bare lies. Simulate what happens on the course. Instead of think- ing about perfect lies, turn the equation round: if you can master pitch shots from bare lies and the rough then when you get a perfect one it will be a breeze!

The chip should be played with any club from a seven iron to a wedge. The address position is the same as a full shot.

ONE MINUTE TIP

Whenever my chipping goes off and I'm striking the ball improperly, I concentrate on keeping my legs as still as possible. There should be no leg movement when you're playing a chip shot. If the legs are still, the arms can move freely back and forth through the ball, thus ensuring the correct contact.

CHIPPING

'I tell them to take 100 chip shots and when they make 100 in a row, we go on to putting.'

American Jackie Burke, on giving golf lessons

Unlike the pitch shot, there is no wrist break during this half-swing. The aim is to keep the ball low to the ground, so a shallow angle of attack is required.

Success, a clean shot! Note the legs have not moved during the shot. The arms have swung in a pendulum movement.

General technique

Chipping and pitching are often mixed up by complete beginners but, after you have read the previous chapter, the difference should be obvious. The chip is played with a straighter-faced club and is designed for the ball to clear a cut of rough and then roll to the pin. Professionals have chipping down to such a fine art that, even when playing to an uneven green with many borrows to negotiate, they always expect to get down in two shots. With a little practice you too should be able to get down in two on many occasions. The chip is one shot in which you need to have a lot of faith in yourself. It's a bread-and-butter shot and will serve you well on far more occasions than the pitch, unless you're playing a course with lots of bunkers and small greens.

It's also a very easy shot to play as it can be played with any club from a seven iron through to a wedge, so select one from your bag. Now, adopt your normal stance, but stand a little closer to the ball and hold the club lightly towards the bottom of the grip. Control is everything with the chip shot and so gripping a little firmer down the shaft will help in this respect.

The ball should be positioned in the middle of your stance and your weight predominantly on your left hand side. Keep your hands ahead of the ball and your knees slightly bent. From this position you will strike the ball on a downward arc which will promote spin and negate any chance of hitting the ground first. Clearly the length of the chip shot will dictate how far you should go on your backswing but you shouldn't have to go back more than 3ft, even for the longest chip. Keep it smooth and rhythmical. No need to worry about unhinging your wrists: the chip is an extension of the putting stroke. Finally, keep your eye on the ball. So many chips are ruined because the player looks to see how he has done before the stroke has been completed and the result is always a destructive thinned shot that invariably scuttles through the green and leaves, at best, exactly the same chip shot coming back.

Here we have two scenarios that can occur around most greens.

Top: If a deep bunker stands between you and the flag, the pitch shot is required, because the chip shot has no height and the ball will nestle in the far end of the bunker.

The greater loft provided by a pitch shot carries the ball over the bunker, enabling it to land softly on the putting surface.

Bottom: The chip shot is the better option here. Nothing stands between the player and the flag so keep the ball close to the ground.

With the pitch shot the margin of error is that much greater. The ball has to land in exactly the right spot to finish close to the pin. It is so easy to leave it either miles short or thin it through the back.

Pitching versus chipping

The headline is perhaps a little misleading, as it suggests that there is a contest between the two and that when you miss a green, you are engaged in a battle of wills between whether to pitch the ball back on to the putting surface or to chip it.

In fact it is not quite like that. If the option to chip the ball is available, then chip it – it's as simple as that. The greater the loft when playing a shot around the green then the greater the chance of error. Let's take a few examples:

a) you've missed the first green by five yards, so now you've got 15 yards to go to the flag with 15ft of rough to negotiate. Pitch or chip? Chip it. Aim to land the ball just on the fringe of the green and let it roll to the pin.

b) You're in heavy rough just off the green with the pin 20 yards away. You're pretty sure that if you took a seven iron, the clubface would become entangled and you would lose control of the shot. Pitch or chip? Chip the ball with a wedge. Make sure you keep your hands ahead of the ball so you're 'chopping' down on it. The grass that will inevitably get between the head of the club and the ball means that it will still roll as if you had played it with a seven iron.

c) A bunker lies between you and the pin, but the face is shallow, so there's no great need of height to get the ball over it. Pitch or chip? Depends on whether there is plenty of green with which to work. If there is, then a chip is your best bet. If not, then pitch it as the extra height will enable you to stop the ball more quickly.

d) A fairly steep, closely-mown bank lies between you and the plateau green with just 10 ft of the putting surface to work with before the flag. Pitch or chip? Chip it up the bank with a six or seven iron, or even a putter if you feel more comfortable with it. The odds on pitching and getting the ball to stop close to the pin are very small and if you miscalculate on the short side, the ball is going to come back and finish at your feet.

QUICK FACT

One of the great chips in recent times was played by Nick Faldo at St Andrews in the first round of the 1990 Open. His drive had finished 40 yards short of the 18th green and many players who had finished in a similar position had opted to pitch the ball into the heart of the green. Not Faldo. He chose a seven iron and played a beautifully executed shot that ran through the Valley of Sin, up the bank, and into the hole for an eagle two. It gave him a 67 and he went on to win the event by five shots.

Left: Another shot that terrifies the high handicapper. Again keep the body still with your weight equally distributed; concentrate on an early wrist break.

Right: This shot is all about conviction. Keep the clubhead moving through the ball; your weight distribution should never alter so avoid the temptation to lean back and scoop.

Buried lie

Playing a pitch shot from a buried lie or deep rough is as much a test of your course management skills as technique. Clearly you are going to lose much of your control over the shot, so what you need to assess is the extent of the trouble that lies between you and the pin and beyond. Is there a bunker to negotiate? A water hazard lurking on the other side of the green?

A bogey from the position in which you have left yourself would not be a disaster, but you do not want to end up with a double bogey or worse. If the lie is bad and there is a water hazard lying in wait, play away from it, even if

it means playing for a part of the green where the flag is not in residence. One of the things to remember about this shot is not to panic and go thrashing at the ball thinking that brute force is the only way to get it out. Unless the lie is truly dire, the basic pitch shot will serve you well enough. Concentrate on your 'half 'n' half' swing and aim to make as clean a contact as you can. Remember to take into account that there will be little spin on the ball, so once it hits the ground it will behave more like a chip shot and roll a considerable distance.

QUICK FACT

There's no denying that the one thing you really need when playing a pitch shot from a buried lie is a bit of luck. Thus did Mark Calcavecchia survive an anxious moment in the 1989 Open at Royal Troon. At the 12th hole he not only had a poor lie, but also a bunker to negotiate. He committed the cardinal sin. His rhythm was jerky and his head was up too quickly. The result was he thinned the shot and was headed for all sorts of trouble on the other side of the green — until the pin got in the way. Calcavecchia's ball finished in the hole for the unlikeliest of birdies and he went on to win the event in a four hole play-off.

Behind a bunker

If a bunker lies between a player and the pin, many people reach automatically for the sand wedge to pitch the ball back on to the green. Yet this shouldn't have to be the case. How steep is the face of the bunker? How much green do you have to work with to the flag? Instead of trying to flop the ball back on to the green and therefore risk flopping it into the sand, a chip with a nine iron or pitching wedge would be a more sensible alternative if the bunker is shallow.

Also, look to see if there is a way you can go around the sand. In the 1976 Open at Birkdale, Severiano Ballesteros announced his arrival to the golfing world with just such a shot. At the 18th hole in the final round, his second shot had put him to the left of the green seemingly with a couple of bunkers to go over and little green with which to work. Yet the Spaniard confirmed his genius by playing a little chip instead through the small channel between the bunkers

to within 3ft of the pin. It looked a miraculous shot, but in fact the option he chose was a far easier one than trying to pitch over the bunkers.

Fringe of the green

Similarly, when on the fringe of the green, most players reach for the putter. In many cases, if the ground in front of them is smooth, this is the correct option. But many will use it even if the ground is rough and then become annoyed when the ball 'takes off' as soon as they hit it. Consider using a five or six iron and chipping the ball using your putting stroke. You don't have to alter anything, but the the ball will carry over the first few feet of rough before rolling to the pin.

ONE MINUTE TIP

When chipping around the green with a five or six iron, consider using not just your putting stroke but a putting grip as well. To do this, rest the index finger of your left hand over the middle fingers of your right hand. This may feel strange at first, but it is a grip that promotes feel, and feel is what this shot is all about.

A small depression or a shallow bunker between a player and the flag and many think automatically: pitch shot. Here is an instance where it doesn't have to be the case.

Clearly there is lots of green to work with and a chip shot is a far better option. A quarter-swing is therefore all that is necessary, cutting down on possible mistakes.

The object is to land the ball on the front of the green and let the ball run out to the hole. Visualise such a scenario in your head and then choose the club which possesses the necessary loft to allow you to carry out the task.

Fred Couples is a master of improvisation. Here he uses the toe end of a Ping putter to lift the ball out of the rough. Seconds later and Fred was celebrating his decision: the ball finished in the hole.

This shot announced the arrival of an astonishing talent on to the world stage. Here, the 19 year old Severiano Ballesteros threads a chip shot between two greenside bunkers at the 18th at Royal Birkdale in the 1976 Open to 4ft. He holed the putt to finish runner-up to Johnny Miller.

ONE MINUTE TIP

When considering what club to use from beyond the fringe of the green, don't forget to include the putter in your options, particularly if you have to get the ball up a steep bank off a tight lie. In circumstances such as this, the putter is often a safe bet: you might not get the ball as close to the pin as you would like, but equally it is unlikely that you will totally mess up.

Which club to chip with?

This is a source of considerable debate within the game: should I chip with a seven iron, nine iron, wedge, sand wedge, or putter? My answer would be to chip with them all (not at the same time, however) and throw in an eight iron for good measure as well.

But not at first. If you are a raw beginner, chip with a seven iron for the first few months. Practise with it in the back garden and learn its trajectory and how hard you need to hit the ball to make it travel a certain distance. Then you can start to experiment.

Many professionals, though, return to chipping with just one club (usually a wedge). They find a certain loss of feel if they swap and change between clubs. Most, though, operate by a hard and fast rule that has stuck for generations: its basic principle is to chip with the club you need to clear the uneven ground before the putting green and allow the ball to roll out to the flag. So, if you're ten feet from the putting surface and the pin is cut 25ft on the green you will need the club which you feel will propel the ball 25ft after landing (probably something like an eight iron). Watch how many professionals abide by this golden rule. Ultimately, however, chip with whichever club you feel most comfortable, as it is absolutely vital to stand over the shot and have total confidence that you are going to hit it close to the pin. If that means chipping with a driver, then so be it, which brings us nicely onto the next topic.

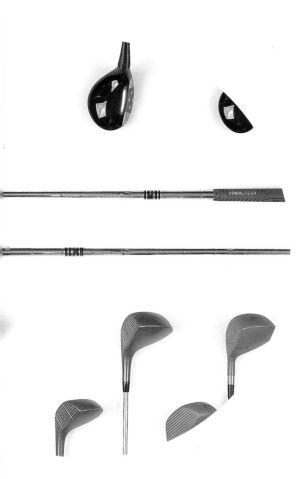

QUICK FACT

In the sudden death play-off for the 1987 Masters, Larry Mize left himself the most difficult of shots after his approach to the 11th green had missed on the left. He had 140ft to go with all sorts of humps and hollows to negotiate and, while conventional wisdom suggested he should pitch the ball most of that distance with a wedge and let the ball run out to the hole, Mize followed his own counsel. He used a seven iron and rolled the ball this way and that, over all the uneven ground, before finally the ball came to rest in the hole for victory. Mize, the local boy, jumped for joy. How good a shot was it? Well, six months on, Mize was invited to try it again. He tried it 100 times. He never came close once.

Alternatives

Fred Couples caused quite a stir at the US Masters a couple of years ago with his solution to a ball that was nesting in a little patch of rough just off the green. Couples chose to use his Ping putter, which was hardly radical although the lie didn't look the sort from which you could use such a club. But when Couples tried a couple of practice swings, it became clear he was going to strike the ball not in the conventional manner but with the toe of the putter.

This caused great excitement among the watching faithful. It caused great excitement all around the world when Couples played the shot to perfection. The toe of the putter eased itself under the ball, which landed on the green very, very gently before trickling down to the flag and into the hole.

A number of players have come up with different answers to different dilemmas, clearly adopting the maxim 'if needs must.' Payne Stewart once used a four wood to play a chip shot where the ball had come to rest on a little tuft of grass beside the green. 'It was as though I was playing it off a tee, so using a wood seemed to be the obvious solution,' Stewart said later. He got down in two.

Many amateurs carry a special chipping iron in their bags, which generally have the same loft as a seven iron but are specifically designed solely for chipping, not for full shots as well.

Many senior players so love hitting their seven woods that they will often chip with the same club. Indeed, golfers have always invented different purposes for clubs than that originally intended. The chip is, in essence, such a simple shot that it was perhaps inevitable that it should attract more than its fair share of experimentation.

There are no rules that say you must play a shot from around the green with either a short iron or a putter. Here, Glen Daly demonstrates that to use a driver you don't have to be standing on a tee.

59

Trying to land pitch shots into an upturned umbrella in the back garden is a marvellous way of improving your technique.

1. As long as your back garden doesn't resemble a wild Borneo jungle, you can easily practise your chipping there. Just ten to fifteen minutes every other day will promote a correct strike of the ball and teach you all you need to know about trajectory and distance. Stick an umbrella in the ground some 20 yards away so you've always got something to aim at.

2. Hopefully the golf club that you use will have a practice putting green that allows you to chip onto it as well. Here you can experiment with different clubs to see which you need for the ball to travel a certain distance once it has landed on the edge of the green.

3. As with pitching, it is very helpful to get into a mental routine before playing a chip shot. The practice ground is where you can learn to commit the following to memory:

a) Is my weight predominantly on my left hand side?

b) Is the ball in the middle of my stance and am I holding the club towards the bottom of the grip?

c) Are my hands ahead of the ball?

d) Have I got a clear picture of what I am trying to achieve with this chip shot?

Here, Sandy Lyle tries to get a mental picture before he beats about the bush.

4. Watch the professionals: Either by viewing on television or attending a tournament in person, to watch the top players do their stuff may be a source of great pleasure but it rarely has anything to do with the game that you play. But around the greens it does, and particularly chip shots. Just watch the way every professional plays this stroke. The weight distribution; the hands ahead of the ball; the smooth controlled rhythm. This is one area of the game where you can not only watch and admire, but realistically seek to emulate as well.

BUNk

Bunkers come in all shapes and sizes.
This one dominates the 4th hole at The
Oxfordshire, stretching for 100 yards.

R SHOTS

Different types of bunkers and sand

Bunkers come in all shapes and sizes, for example at the Oxfordshire, where this book was photographed, the par five 4th hole features a bunker that is 100 yards long by 45 yards wide. At the short par four 14th there is a pot bunker that is barely wide enough to swing a club.

Bunkers have long been steeped in mystique and the best of them are the stuff of legend. At many of the old links courses they have names and at the Old Course at St Andrews the vast majority of them do, the most famous of them being the Road Hole bunker, a vast deep pit that protects half of the green at the 17th, the Road Hole. Some people refer to it as the Sands of Nakajima, after the unfortunate Japanese Tommy Nakajima who fell from grace in the 1978 Open after needing four shots to extricate himself.

At the 14th, Hell Bunker stands some 100 yards short of the green. It dates back to 1882 when one golfer, after a terrible round, complained to the St Andrews professional, Old Tom Morris, that the only decent lie he had was at the bottom of the deep bunker at the 14th, where he used a wood to get out. Morris, who didn't have much of a sense of humour at the best of times, is said to have despatched a work crew there and then with the words, 'Come hell or high water, dig it so deep that no player will ever use a wood from there again'.

The original intention was that finishing in a bunker would cost a player a shot, but after Gene Sarazen invented the sand wedge, golfers began to save par with great regularity. Today, it has reached the stage where a normal bunker shot strikes no fear at all in the top professional, who will expect nine times out of ten to get down in two.

This in turn has led to modern courses featuring more severe bunkers and contrived sand traps and it seems the only man who has lost out is the humble amateur who wasn't so enamoured with the conventional ones let alone those of a more intricate variety.

Yet, given the correct technique and a modicum of confidence, no player should take more than three shots to complete a hole from a greenside bunker. With today's equipment, anything worse than a bogey from a decent lie in the sand is a poor score indeed.

One of the most famous hazards in golf is the Church Pews bunker on the third hole at Oakmont, Pennsylvania. It certainly proved too much for an ageing Arnold Palmer during the 1994 US Open.

QUICK FACT

One of the most famous bunker shots of recent times was made by Bob Tway in the 1986 USPGA Championship at Inverness, Ohio. Playing the last hole, the American was tied with Greg Norman, but found a trap with his second shot. A play-off seemed the most likely scenario, with Norman an obvious favourite to win if it was all settled in normal time. That plot didn't take into account Tway's powers from the sand. He played the perfect shot, the ball landing 12ft from the pin before finishing in the hole.

The ball should be positioned in the middle of the stance with the clubface slightly open.

ONE MINUTE TIP

There's an easy way to learn how much sand to take: draw a line in the sand two inches behind the ball and two inches in front of it. Both these lines should be obliterated in order to play the shot properly. Of course you can only do this in practice: you're not allowed to touch the sand with your club or your finger under normal circumstances. One other thing which can't be stressed enough – make sure you complete the follow-through and swing smoothly through the ball. Conquer that fear!

Technique

Like the pitch shot, playing from a bunker is 20% technique and 80% confidence. Show me a golfer who regularly has trouble from the sand and I'll show you someone who hasn't mastered the basic fundamentals of playing the shot, yet they're so straightforward that an hour's practice from a bunker will do much to remove the fear from someone terrified of going into a sand trap.

The basic technique is this: make sure the ball is positioned in the centre of your stance; your feet and your shoulders should be open, that is pointing a little to the left of the target; make sure you have a firm stance in the bunker, and that the blade of the club is a little open as well.

What you are trying to do from now on is a half swing, as in the pitch shot. You're aiming to hit the sand some two inches behind the ball – you want to take a clean layer of sand, not dig for Great Britain, so don't thrash at it – just swing normally, but imagine that you're trying to swing an inch below the ball. One cardinal sin the amateur makes in a bunker is quitting on the shot; you must complete a full rhythmical follow-through for successful results. If you

have a longer bunker shot to play – say, about 30 yards – then you should hit the sand just one inch behind the ball using a three-quarter swing. The key to good bunker play is possessing the confidence to descend into the bunker knowing that at worst it will come out and at best it will finish close to the hole. Good technique will help you nurture that confidence.

When practising your bunker play, draw a line in the sand to the left of the intended target, this will ensure that you achieve the necessary open stance.

This enables you to swing the club from out-to-in, promoting a soft landing for the ball as it hits the green; the object is to hit two inches behind the sand, so draw another line in the sand at that point.

Take a half to three-quarter backswing and make sure you complete the follow-through.

Downhill lie

Finishing in the back of a bunker, contemplating a downhill lie, is an unhappy experience. If the green to which you are playing is small and there's trouble behind, then what you're left with is one of the hardest shots in the game. The most important thing to remember is not to let your fear show when you enter the bunker. Be in a positive frame of mind, believing that the ball is going to come out and stay on the green. Occasionally, if the back wall of the bunker is steep, you will find yourself unable to make a proper back-swing and in this case you will either have to take an unplayable or come out sideways.

It, however, would be extremely unfortunate, as normally you would be able to take a swipe at it. Position the ball a little further back in your stance to take account of the slope, but otherwise visualise, as normal, hitting the sand about two inches behind the ball. Here, more than ever, it is important to keep everything smooth and complete the follow-through.

Uphill lie

An uphill lie presents a completely different set of circumstances. Here it shouldn't be any trouble at all getting the ball out of the sand. However, the problem is getting sufficient distance to get the ball to the flag, because the slope will act as a launch pad and send it straight into the air. Instead, position the ball a little further forward in your stance, but otherwise swing normally. If the pin is a long way away then consider a three-quarters swing or using a pitching wedge to compensate.

Top: One of the most difficult shots in the game, and the most important thing here is to maintain your balance. So widen your stance, with the ball towards the front foot.

Centre: The wrists break quickly to avoid catching the back lip of the bunker. Take a half-backswing.

Bottom: It's all about having confidence in your ability now. A smooth follow-through, making sure you don't 'quit' on the shot, will ensure you get the ball out of the bunker without too much damage done.

Top: Again, take a slightly wider stance than normal for this shot. The ball should be positioned towards the front foot.

Centre: Here, the backswing should be three-quarters in length, because from an uphill lie the ball will ascend rapidly, with consequent loss of distance.

Bottom: This is actually an easy shot if the flag is cut close to the bunker. If distance is required then play it with a pitching wedge.

ONE MINUTE TIP

Gary Player is widely regarded as the best bunker player of all time. The reason? He spent long hours practising his technique until his confidence was such that getting down in two became a formality and that more often than not he would be trying to hole the shot. When this occurred with some frequency it caused resentment among some opponents who thought the little South African was blessed with more than his fair share of good fortune. Player's answer? 'You may be right but do you know something? The more I practise the luckier I get.'

Fried eggs are not good for you. Not at breakfast time, nor on the golf course either. But don't enter the bunker feeling the shot is impossible. It is far from that.

QUICK FACT

In some countries, and particularly in America, you will see huge bunkers known as waste bunkers on the sides of some fairways. These are the only bunkers where you are allowed to ground your club prior to beginning your stroke. You will know whether you are in a waste bunker by looking at the local rules on the back of the scorecard, which will identify them as such.

Occasionally you may be the victim of another player's thoughtlessness and finish in a footprint. If there is plenty of sand in the bunker, eliminate the circumstances from your mind and play a normal explosion shot.

Fried egg lie

We've all experienced that sinking feeling: an iron shot heading for a bunker is bad enough, but when it gets there, it falls like a stone from the sky and ends up in a plugged lie: the fried egg, as it is known.

To those players who are scared of bunkers anyway, this is a nightmare unfolding before their eyes. They flail at the ball with no real conception of how it is going to come out and of course it doesn't. Their confidence is so shattered that the next one probably doesn't come out either.

Using a wedge is always a good idea in these circumstances. It will cut through the sand more easily. Otherwise, the only other difference is to have a slightly fuller swing than you would normally use for a bunker shot of similar distance from a good lie. Remember too, that when the ball hits the green, it will have no spin on it and so it will roll forever.

Note how, in a fried egg situation, the stance is not open but the feet are pointing towards the target. Take a wedge as it cuts more easily through the sand. You need a smooth, half backswing.

There's no need to try to force the ball out; the club is designed to cope with this sort of situation. And one thing you can be sure of is that the ball will roll once it lands on the green.

Footprint lie

Equally distressing is the ball that finishes in a footprint. Here, once more, a wedge may be your best option, depending upon how heavy the culprit was and how deep his footprint. If the ball is a fair way down, then use a wedge. Once more a positive attitude will work wonders here – you have the equipment to extricate the ball from such a situation, so don't enter the bunker thinking you have to swing yourself off your feet to get it out. You don't.

Severiano Ballesteros is the modern genius from bunkers. No doubt it helped that he learned the game playing on a beach near his home in Pedrena.

ONE MINUTE TIP

If using a putter out of the sand, remember that you will need to hit the ball considerably harder than normal. Obviously don't go to extremes and thrash at it as you would a driver, but even if the sand is hard, it will slow the ball. So imagine that you are putting under the same resistance as if you were putting on your back lawn — always presuming, of course, that your back lawn is neither a bowling green nor untamed!

Wet sand

After long spells of rain, the sand in a bunker will obviously be wet and hard and exhibit different properties than when under normal circumstances. When you step into the bunker and go to take your stance, you will be able to gauge how hard the sand is and, if it has compacted, then a wedge will probably be a more suitable club. The reason is that the flange at the bottom of the sand wedge has been designed for use under circumstances that will prevail at least 90% of the time.

However, if the sand has compacted, then the flange will bounce off it and you will hit the ball without being able to get underneath it. The result will be a thinned shot into the face of the bunker – either that or a thinned shot that clears the face of the bunker and finishes in a hedge or someone's back garden. By contrast, the thinner leading edge of the wedge will allow you to cut through the compacted sand and play a bunker shot in the orthodox way. The only difference is that the wedge doesn't have as much loft and so the ball will come out on a flatter trajectory and will roll further.

Shallow-faced bunker

Many players just automatically reach for a sand wedge when their ball finishes in a bunker, even if the trap has little or no lip to it. Their reasoning is: 'I am in sand therefore logically I must use a sand wedge'. And maybe it does, but think a little here. If the ball is lying well in the sand and it is not of the fluffy kind that will stop the ball rolling, why not consider using a putter?

After all, what is to stop you? If the lip is low enough it will not stop the ball coming out and if the sand is firm, then the ball will roll. One thing to remember, of course, is that you will not be able to ground your putter behind the ball, just as you cannot ground your sand wedge.

Wet, compacted sand can render a sand wedge
totally unsuitable for getting out of a bunker.
Use your pitching wedge, or even a putter if the
bunker has no front lip.

Putters come in all shapes and sizes these days and it is vital to choose one that gives you an air of confidence when you step on to the greens.

CHECKLIST

1. When you take your usual address position does the putter square up naturally to the ball?

2. When you strike a putt out of the sweetspot does it roll much further than a mistimed putt?

3. Is the putter the right length? Are you able to assume your normal address position?

4. Did you hole a goodly proportion of putts on the practice putting green?

PUTTING

Choosing a putter

Passing on advice for choosing a putter is almost like offering tips on selecting your ideal partner or what car to drive. I guess what I'm trying to say is that, in the end, much of it comes down to personal opinion.

As a result, when you enter your local golf emporium, you will be terribly spoilt for choice. Putters with exotic names – Nick Price won the 1994 USPGA Championship using one called 'The Fat Lady' (I bet it was a fat man who came up with the name). You'll see putters with short heads, putters with long heads, putters with straight heads, putters with triangular-shaped heads, putters with bulbous heads, putters with heads that have no frills at all.

Putters with broomhandle shafts, putters with thick grips, putters with . . . well I'm sure you've got the picture by now.

Putting is such a psychological game that looks do matter. You need to like what you see. When you pick it up, it must feel the correct weight to you. Now take your stance behind the ball – does it sit nicely and enable you to line up to your target without having to make any adjustments?

Most important of all, when you strike a couple of putts is the ball coming naturally out of the sweetspot? Thinking cheaply can be a very expensive business when it comes to buying a putter. You need one where you can find the sweetspot easily and when you strike it properly the ball rolls freely and fully, otherwise you'll be discarding it quickly and having to buy another one. If you're fairly new to the game, forget all thoughts of anything too fancy. Don't think about broomhandle putters for instance, or putters with thick grips.

When Jack Nicklaus won the 1986 Masters, he did so with a putter that had an unusually large head, easily twice the normal size. MacGregor, the company to whom Nicklaus was signed at the time, soon had a version on the market, and it sold in the hundreds and thousands. But I bet hardly anyone is using one now, ten years on – Nicklaus certainly isn't, so beware of anything flash, any gimmicks.

Make sure as well that it is the right length for you. When you take your stance and hold the club your body should fall naturally into the address position. If you are scrunched over the ball, then the shaft is too short for you. If you have to stand like a guardsman, then it is clearly too long.

On the question of weight, this is something that is of personal preference but ideally you want to steer clear of anything too lightweight because your timing will be affected and consequently the quality of strike will be impaired.

Finally, don't expect to find your ideal putting partner in the first place you look. Indeed you may find yourself going through several relationships before you find the one for you. It may be the grandest thing in the shop or it may be completely plain and fuss-free, but what is vital is that you get along just fine. And if that is the case care for it, cherish it through the good times – and don't go looking for a divorce at the first sign of trouble.

Remember that grasping the art of putting will save you a countless number of shots every time you play. So spend some time practising.

QUICK FACT

You'd think a psychology degree would have helped Tom Watson come to terms with a decade of bad putting wouldn't you? And in a way I suppose you could say it did, as it enabled him to analyse what had gone wrong and why he had deteriorated from being the best putter from 6 foot to becoming, under pressure, just about the worst. But having broken it all down and analysed where it went wrong, could he put all the pieces back together again? Could the man who won eight major championships between 1975 to 1983 win any after the magic had gone? Alas no. A psychology degree is clearly no match for the mighty forces at work with putting.

General technique

Bobby Locke, Billy Casper and Isao Aoki, to pick three players from different generations, would all have had the book thrown at them if there was only one way to putt. The fact that they were three of the best putters of all time fully illustrates that anything goes in putting if it's legal and it works.

Aoki may have been the worst. The manual tells you that the putter head should lie square on the ground; the toe of Aoki's putter hung proudly in the air, as if it was gasping for breath. The manual tells you that the wrists should be firm throughout the stroke; Aoki so cocked his wrists it was as though he was playing a backhand at tennis.

If you saw Aoki on the practice putting green, you'd have told him to start again from scratch. Well, you would have if you had told him before he started holing putts from all over the place.

There's one at every club, too, and maybe more than one: golfers who defy all conventional putting laws, yet consistently hole out from every square inch of every green.

To a certain extent then, putting is God-given: that seems to be the lesson here. But for the less gifted among us, there are rules that ought to be followed for consistency in this most infuriating area of the sport.

There are perhaps just two basic tenets to putting: the wrists should stay firm throughout the stroke, and the stroke itself should be smooth and rhythmical.

The stroke is often compared to the pendulum movement on a grandfather clock and that is probably the best analogy of all. The other thing to remember is that the rest of the body should remain perfectly still throughout the putting stroke. That is not to say that you should be thinking you are a statue and freeze on the spot. Any tension and almost certainly your putting will go to pot. When you are about to stand over a putt, try to relax your body and then concentrate your mind on the ball, moving your arms as if they were that pendulum. Mastered all that? Now the hard part begins – learning to read the greens and the different borrows, as well as coping with the immense amount of psychology at work.

The ball should be lined up opposite the middle of the putter head at address.

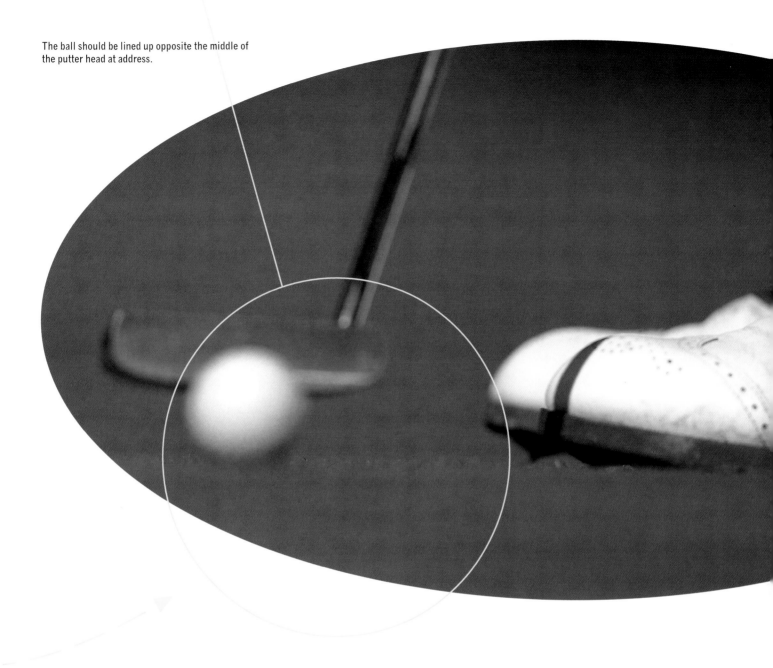

Although many different methods of putting have won major championships, the one that works for most golfers involves no wrist break and is known as the pendulum method.

What you are trying to achieve is the same motion as the pendulum movement on a grandfather clock. The length of backswing depends on the length of putt: clearly, the longer the putt the longer the backswing.

The head remains motionless throughout, the eyes fixed on the ball, but don't tense up. And remember: absolutely no breaking of the wrists!

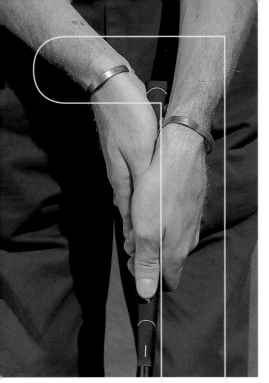

On the pro circuit it has now become fashionable to putt with the left hand below the right. Many players feel this prevents any wrist-break, although you should persevere with more orthodox methods before falling back on this one.

Putting grips

Given that putting is often considered a game within a game, it is appropriate that a little playing around with the accepted wisdom is allowed here. No-one is going to stand opposite you, studying your grip on the greens, tut-tutting: 'well I'm sorry this will not do,' as they might if they spotted something awry on the tee.

There's never been a golfer born who has not struggled at some point to get the ball in the hole and experimented as a result with different methods in an effort to find the key. In the end, however, many golfers settle on one of the methods photographed here. The first two methods are most popular, while the third illustrates putting's boundless possibilities.

The first is the orthodox grip that most players use from tee to green. Perhaps they're working on the principle: heck, it took me long enough to feel comfortable with this method without trying to get used to another one.

Or: it's working from tee to green, why not on the green as well?

There's certainly an obvious logic to using an orthodox grip and it represents a good starting point.

What every golfer is after is the feeling that the hands are in control of the putter head. Instead of the left index finger forming an interlocking grip, many players find that by placing it over the fingers of the right hand, as in photograph two, they can achieve this feel, because the grip is now less rigid. This is perhaps the most popular method of all and the one most used by the top professionals.

The third photograph illustrates what can only be described as the Langer method. Be warned: the German only alighted on this drastic solution after three bouts of the putting yips and following experiments with a whole host of other methods.

Langer has received literally thousands of letters over the years from other sufferers, all enclosing their cure. In the end he came up with his own, although several players, including Sandy Lyle and Roger Davis, have both experimented with it since. Not for long, though. The master remains the ultimate pupil.

'If you three putt the first green, they will never remember it. But if you three putt the 18th they will never forget it.'

Walter Hagen.

'When I putt, my emotions collide like
tectonic plates. It has left my memory
circuits full of scars that will not heal.'

The inimitable American, Mac O'Grady.

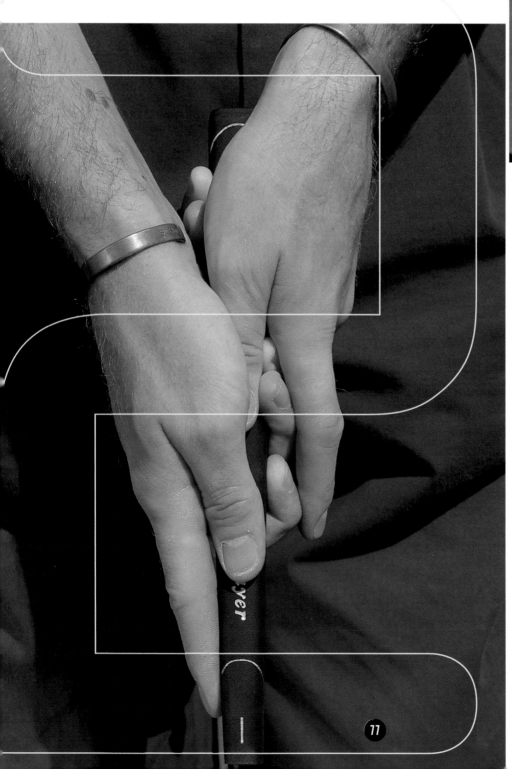

Left: A popular variation on the orthodox
grip. The forefinger of the left hand has
simply been withdrawn from the grip
itself to promote a greater sense of feel.
The index finger of the right hand can
either remain closed around the grip or,
as in this case, point downwards.

Top: The Langer method, or perhaps it
should be known as the last resort grip.
Langer has certainly made it work for him
but you really need to have exhausted all
possibilities before you follow his lead.

'My putting is so bad that I could putt off
a tabletop and still leave the ball halfway
down the leg.'

JC Snead

Reading greens

Once a golfer has mastered the general technique of putting and settled on a method that promotes feel, the next thing to conquer is how to actually get the ball into the hole. It is one thing to strike the putts correctly and have a good idea of distance. But the ball will still not regularly fall into a small hole unless a player can read the greens.

Sadly, this is a skill gained more by experience than anything else. If you play most of your golf at the same course then you will learn over time the subtleties that exist in those particular greens and master them – well, some of the time anyway.

The hard and fast rule to observe is that the golf ball will always follow the laws of Newton. So, if you are putting downhill it is going to travel much faster than in the opposite direction. If a borrow stands between your ball and the hole, then allowances have to be made according to its severity. On page 80 our professional, Scott Cranfield, is trying to negotiate a sizeable borrow on the 13th green at the Oxfordshire. See how far to the left he has had to aim to accommodate the slope. This is partly because of its size but also because the greens are slick and smooth. The better the greens the more allowance has to be made for borrow. Wet and windy conditions can make quite a difference to putting. If the greens are sodden then the borrows will not have nearly the same effect as if they were dry. As a rough guide, allow perhaps half the borrow you would normally.

If you are putting downwind, inevitably the putt will be quicker than if putting in the opposite direction. The difference can be quite dramatic when the putt is both downhill and downwind. Approach such putts with extreme caution.

Many beginners are always puzzled as to why a top professional studies a putt from all angles, assessing it from behind the hole and also back behind the ball, and occasionally side-on as well.

What they are trying to assess, in addition to the borrows, is the direction of the grain of the grass. If you are studying the putt from behind your ball and the grass looks shiny then this means the grain is with you and the putt will be quicker than if the grass has a matt finish, which means the grain is against.

Dear Beginner, you'll be pleased to know that greens these days are invariably cut not just in parallel lines but across too, in order to gain a greater consistency and lessen the importance of grain. So don't lose any sleep over it.

Above: Remember that when putting uphill you will always need to hit the ball that much harder than for a straight putt.

Left: Sam Snead never had any problems reading the greens, yet putting was always perceived as his Achilles' heel. Mind you, it did not prevent him winning 81 times on the US tour, which is not only a record but pretty good for a supposedly poor putter.

'I enjoy the oohs and aahs from the gallery
when I hit my drives.
But I'm getting pretty tired of the awws and
uhhs when I miss the putt.'

John Daly

Here, a slope is clearly visible between ball and
flag and, just as the land falls from left to right, so
will the ball. When the greens are fast, aim well
left of the flag.

Only experience will teach you how hard to hit
the ball and how much to allow. But don't get
disheartened. This is one of the easier skills in the
game to acquire.

The putter –
your flexible friend

Professionals spend so much time practising these days it is little wonder they
indulge in some outrageous experiments. At one tournament I remember
watching Fred Couples play an iron shot that eventually finished just a couple
of inches off the green, but in a nasty collar of rough.

What to do now? He could have played the obvious flop wedge shot. He
played a rehearsal shot with it, but was clearly worried that the wide face of the
wedge would become tangled in the rough and affect the impact.

So instead he got out his Ping putter. Gasps of disbelief went round the
gallery. How on earth was he going to putt the ball out of deep rough? Couples
had the answer: he was not. Not by a conventional method anyway. He turned
the putter on its side so now, rather than having a club with a wide face
swishing through the rough, he had the narrowest one imaginable.

He played the shot to perfection. The edge of the putter collided with the
bottom of the ball and it dropped gently on to the green, meandered down
towards the flag before falling into the hole.

Don't be afraid to use the putter for other shots if the situation allows it. Here the front lip of the bunker is non-existent and so the putter is a viable option.

It was the shot of a master craftsman, of course, but it underlined the flexibility that exists with a putter. It doesn't have to be used just on the putting green. It can be used from a greenside bunker if the face of the sand trap possesses a shallow lip (just remember not to ground it when addressing the ball). Sometimes it is more useful than a seven iron or a wedge from just off the green. I've seen players finish in front of the terrifying Road Hole bunker on the 17th at St Andrews with seemingly no room to negotiate between the trap and the flag. But great golf holes are always designed with an escape route in mind and here the key is the contours of the bunker. The less skilful players ignored them and pitched for the back of the green and settled for a bogey five. But the talented chose their putters, using the contours of the bunker to bring the ball back towards the hole to set up the chance of a par.

The lesson demonstrated here is that, while the putter is the only acceptable club to use on the greens, it is far from the only place where it is acceptable to employ it.

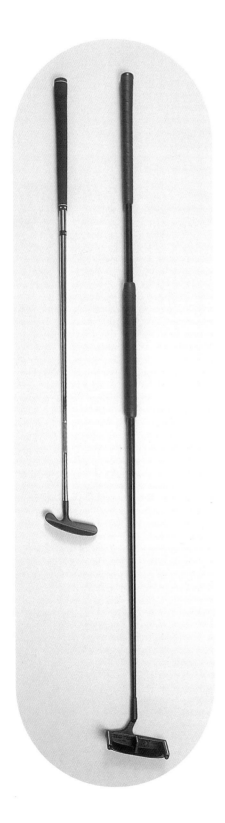

Alternative styles

The putt that won the historic 1985 Ryder Cup at the Belfry, the first time that a team from Europe, as opposed to Great Britain and Ireland, had triumphed against the Americans, was an absolute beauty.

Perhaps you can picture it in your mind's eye: Sam Torrance on the 18th green against Andy North – look at those firm wrists through the stroke and the gorgeous pendulum action and, yards from the hole, there is no doubt that the ball is going to disappear below ground. Yet five years later Torrance had abandoned that stroke, that pendulum movement. He was using a broomhandle putter that should have been banned if the Royal & Ancient had followed its own rules – just how does a broomhandle putter square with the rule that says all clubs should be of a similar likeness? Then again, it is just as well for the Scot that they didn't, for he declared that he would have had to have given up the game if forced to go back to a conventional method.

Alternative putting is nothing new. Another Sam, Snead of that ilk, was putting with a croquet style towards the end of his career, until the United States Golf Association, the game's ruling body in America, declared it to be unlawful. No doubt if Snead was playing competitively today he would have filed and won a multi-million dollar lawsuit for loss of earnings and the emotional hurt.

Once the croquet stance was outlawed, players turned to gripping the club differently. Nowadays many right-handed golfers hold the club using a left-hander's grip: that is, with left hand below right. The elusive thing that they are all trying to recapture is that vital pendulum movement – putting with the left hand below the right is supposed to encourage the hinging of the wrists and a smooth stroke.

With the broomhandle putter, the broomhandle is the pendulum and all Torrance's hands are doing is keeping the pendulum on the right path. Many people, including Tom Watson, think it should be banned for that reason, quite apart from the other, more obvious one. In the R&A's premises at St Andrews they keep a vast selection of all the clubs that have been banned over the years and by far the largest representation is what you might term alternative putters. Putters with wing mirrors, putters with sight lines to look down, croquet putters . . . the list is a tribute to the imagination of man and his powers of invention. It is also a journey into a black hole, to seek a putter that cures all ills. You may as well look for something that enables a football striker to put the ball in the back of the net every time he kicks the ball.

The broomhandle putter has grown in popularity and here you can see how it acquired its name, as the shaft is far longer than normal.

Right: Sam Snead was still a marvellous golfer well into his sixties but the problem was that his putting didn't keep up. He tried everything, even resorting at one stage to a croquet style. The United States Golf Association called time on that one, declaring it illegal.

Below: Sam Torrance is in no doubt that the broomhandle putter saved his career from oblivion. Six years on he remains its best exponent.

ONE MINUTE TIP

With all these putters from which to choose, it might be instructive to learn what the best practitioners of the art have selected. I think the two best putters I have seen are Bob Charles and Ben Crenshaw. And Charles always used a plain bull's-eye putter that was free of any etchings or markings. And Crenshaw used, nay still uses, a plain blade putter that was given to him while he was at college. Do you think a lesson here might be that putting has more to do with the person than the tool he is using, rather than the other way round, which seems to be how it is promoted by the manufacturers?

Bernhard Langer has certainly suffered for his art. Three times he has had the yips – and yet each time he has come back.

84

The yips is an involuntary stab at the ball, caused by the hands acting independently of the brain. There's nothing sadder than watching a player so inflicted.

The yips - golf's deadly disease

It is impossible to believe that there is a more distressing word in the golfer's lexicon. It is a horrible sounding word for a horrible disease and dear old Henry Longhurst's belief – 'once you got 'em you've always got 'em' – has proved sadly true in the case of thousands of golfers. Longhurst, of course, should have known. He so suffered from the yips that eventually he gave up the game because of them.

Is there any cure for the yips? The television commentator Peter Alliss didn't think so either and it was the crushing onslaught of this condition under pressure that prevented him from ever fulfilling a great talent as a player.

What is it? Basically it is the total breakdown in communication between the brain and the hands. Players have been known to stand over putts unable to take the club back from the ball.

One of the worst sufferers was Harry Vardon, despite the fact that he won the Open on a record six occasions. In his book *How to Play Golf,* he gave a vivid description: 'As I stood addressing the ball, I would watch for my right hand to jump. At the end of two seconds, I would not be looking at the ball at all. My gaze would be riveted on my right hand. I simply could not resist the desire to see what it was going to do. Directly, as I felt that it was about to jump, I would snatch at the ball in a desperate effort to play the shot before the involuntary movement could take effect . . . '

In the 1988 Open at Lytham, Bernhard Langer, the most famous sufferer in recent times, struck the most marvellous second shot to the 17th, leaving himself with just an 8ft putt for a three. He walked off the green with an eight, having needed four putts from 2ft. When the yips strike, there is nothing you can do.

Langer reckoned that in his case the yips was due to putting on poor greens in Germany as a young man. When he was making a name for himself in his teens, he would quite regularly need 40 putts to complete a round and it was a tribute to his consummate ball-striking and his natural tenacity that nonetheless people still talked of his being a future star.

Yet the Langer story is also one of hope and proof that ultimately Longhurst was wrong. For Langer has had the yips three times and beat them every time. And how he beat them . . . in the 1993 Masters he won the event for a second time and over the notoriously difficult Augusta greens three-putted just once in 72 holes.

QUICK FACT

In America a couple of years ago a wealthy golfer offered a $20,000 reward for anyone who came up with something that cured him of the yips. The fellow that suggested giving up the game may have been on to something, but unsurprisingly didn't collect the loot. But of the thousands of remedies suggested one did work. . . and the wealthy businessman happily handed over the cash.

THE RULES

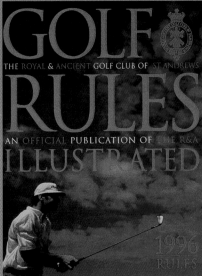

Four of the great names in golf. But all have been involved in rules controversies at one time or another during their careers.

In recent years the Royal and Ancient have striven to make the rules more accessible. This excellent illustrated guide is perhaps the best example.

'There is only one way to play the game. You might as well praise a man for not robbing a bank.'

The great American golfer Bobby Jones, after penalising himself a shot and losing the 1925 US Open by a one stroke margin.

History and Background

Back then it was all so simple. In 1744, when a group of men from the Honourable Company of Edinburgh Golfers got together to draw up a list of governing rules, they felt the necessity to come up with only a handful of regulations. Two hundred and fifty-odd years later and how different things have become. For nearly all that time the rules drawn up by the Royal and Ancient Golf Club of St Andrews have been considered the backbone of the game. Over that time, they have made over one hundred and thirty thousand separate adjudications as people have written in with examples of the game's list of possible variations.

In theory, what we have now are just 34 rules, but in practice each of them brings sheet after sheet of clauses and sub-clauses. They have a life of their own and as new judgements are made, so they change. It is a growth industry.

'They are the equivalent of a complex jigsaw puzzle,' is R&A Rules Secretary John Glover's explanation. Hands up if you know all the rules of golf? I bet no more than one golfer in 750 could answer that honestly and still raise their hand.

Certainly not the tournament professionals. They're a dead loss. They're always falling foul of one obscure rule or another. Hardly a tournament goes by without someone being disqualified for unwittingly breaking the law. Nick Faldo, for example. Given his precise approach to the game, you would think he would know them backwards wouldn't you? Faldo broke two rules in two separate tournaments in 1994 alone.

Yet, you've got to have some sympathy for the pros. The most heartbreaking example of all came in 1967 when the Argentinian, Roberto de Vicenzo, birdied the 17th hole to tie Bob Goalby and so force a play-off in the US Masters.

That is what happened and in any other sport the act itself would be enough. But not in golf. The player himself has to record all his strokes on a scorecard and when he has signed it, then it becomes a binding contract. De Vicenzo signed for a four on that fateful 17th hole and under the rules of the game the higher score had to stand. Do cry for me, Argentina.

You have to feel sorry for the pros too, in the way that every step they take and every move they make is covered by television and beamed back into the homes of smart alecs who like nothing more than the thought of tripping up the pros.

A few years ago, as Tom Watson and Lee Trevino walked from a green to the next tee during a tournament, their conversation was picked up by a microphone. Watson was telling Trevino how to cure a fault. Can't do that, Tom. A viewer rang in to complain that Watson was giving advice. The complaint was upheld. Watson was penalised.

History and background (continued)

And yet for all the importance to the beginner of lessons from a club pro, equally, no golfer should be allowed out on to a course until he has a working knowledge of the rules. That's as much for his own benefit as anyone else's.

John L Low wrote in 1912, 'Some men have a mutual spirit with the game, and, though they know nothing about the rules of golf, they never have any difficulty in knowing the proper thing to do when some perplexing situation arises.'

What was true in 1912 is palpably not the case now. Say you slice your drive and it comes to rest against a fence that surrounds a clump of trees. Do you just go ahead and play it? Isn't that the proper thing to do? After all, you hit it there. No it isn't. The fence is considered an immovable obstruction and you are allowed to lift and drop your ball without penalty, and now you can play straight for the green.

What if your ball comes to rest against a chopped tree trunk? That's just tough isn't it? Well, actually it isn't. It's considered 'ground under repair' and that's another stroke you've saved.

Professional players have raised this kind of interpretation to an art form. They're always looking for line-of-sight rulings from television gantries and the like. Jack Nicklaus once insisted that the rope between two out-of-bounds posts be lowered over his golf ball to determine whether enough of it was in bounds for him to play. It was, and he won the tournament.

So, forget Low and remember Nicklaus's own words, 'Golf was never meant to be a fair game. There is no common justice. There never can be.'

There speaks the man who mastered the art of playing on seaside courses where a dependency on luck of the bounce has driven so many others to distraction; who has accepted that a putt that shaves the hole instead of dropping in is not an act of fate but part of a brutal sport. Learning the rules can help you plot your way through this minefield of a game.

And if you think the rules of golf are unfathomable now, you should have tried learning them 100 years ago. Then it looked as if St Andrews might lose its authority to rule over the game. This was because the sport itself was in turmoil, as most clubs played to rules suitable only for their own terrain. The R&A themselves had a rule that referred to the procedures for recovery from the 'station master's garden.'

Only the Royal Isle of Wight club, with a small nine hole course near Bembridge harbour, framed a set of rules to 'suit all greens,' and they received considerable support. So much in fact, that it seemed this modest seaside club might usurp the authority of the R&A themselves.

As soon as the first bunker was dug and the first green mown
people began compiling rules for golf. This early rule book is
on display at the St Andrews museum.

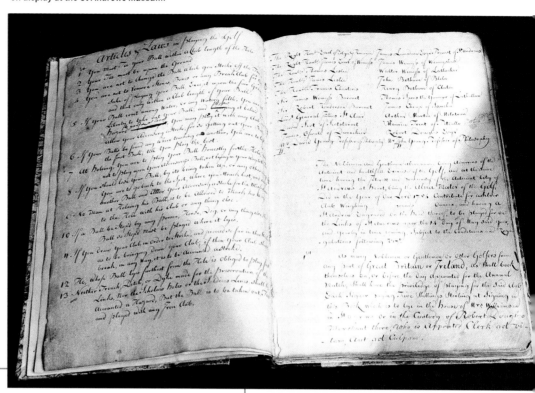

'Golf was never meant to be a fair game. There
is no common justice. There never can be.'

Jack Nicklaus

Jack Nicklaus was always a great stickler
for the rules and he was never afraid to
use them to his advantage.

Top left: If a water hazard has dried up there is nothing in the rules to stop a golfer playing his shot from it. Although in some countries it may be wise to check that there are no large reptiles impeding your lie.

Top right: Dress codes are invariably in operation when watching or playing golf. This Spanish notice needs no translation.

Bottom left: Honesty is everything in golf. Unlike in some other sports we could mention.

Bottom right: Peter Baker underlined the game's integrity when he penalised himself a shot on the 18th hole in the 1985 Amateur Championship, even though he knew it would cost him his match.

'If a ball comes to rest in dangerous proximity to a hippopotamus or crocodile, another ball may be dropped at a safe distance, no nearer the hole, without penalty.'

Local rule, Nyanza Golf Club, Africa

History and background (continued)

A clear example of the once chaotic state of the rules is indicated by the different interpretations that applied if you lost your ball. At St Andrew's, it was loss of hole. At the Royal Isle of Wight you hit another from near the place where it was lost and added two strokes. At Hoylake and Westward Ho! it was to go back, losing stroke and distance.

The St Andrews rule was eventually abandoned because it was too harsh, as was the Bembridge law, which left the Hoylake rule as followed today. St Andrews was declared the sole arbiter of the game because there was a fear that if that authority was handed to the Isle of Wight, the game would polarise into Scottish and English rules. Sadly, the Royal Isle of Wight club no longer even exists. It closed in 1962, and its fairways are now open to the public for picnics. One final point. The most important point of all, in fact. Golf is the ultimate game of integrity. I've seen Peter Baker lose a quarter-final match in the Amateur Championship because he, and he alone, saw his ball move one quarter of an inch as he addressed his second shot to the 18th hole. Harsh it may seem, but Baker felt obliged to point this out to the referee, knowing that he would have no option but to penalise him the stroke that cost him the game.

In every other sport, it's a case of what you can get away with, but not in golf. Knowing the rules is every golfer's responsibility because he is the sole arbiter of his actions. If people don't know the rules they are liable to break them, and it's a fine line that separates breaking them deliberately and breaking them through ignorance. The former are cheats of course, and those caught have had their lives ruined because their peers are of the opinion that if they can cheat at golf, they can cheat at anything. So know the rules. It is no exaggeration to say the game's future reputation depends on it.

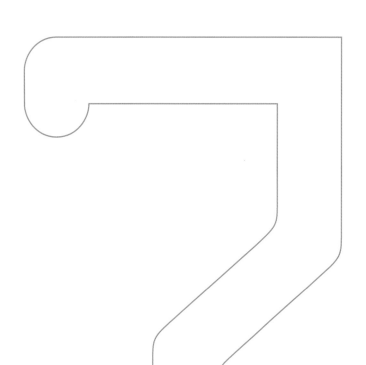

The basic rules of golf

Here are the rules of which you should have a working knowledge before stepping out on to the golf course.

Rule 7

Practice: After four-putting the 6th green you are quite entitled to try each putt again to see what the hell went wrong, provided there is no-one waiting in the middle of the fairway to play their shots. As you come off the green you can chip your way to the 7th tee if you want, providing again that you are not causing undue delay. What you are not allowed to do is practise on the course prior to playing any stroke-play competition round, nor are you permitted to walk out and test the putting surfaces of any green. If it is a 36-hole competition, no practice on the course between rounds is permitted (you'd have to be very fit, mind, to even want to).

Rule 8

Advice: It is the most natural scenario in the world: you're standing on the tee at the short 11th and the person against whom you are playing has hit a gorgeous shot, right over the flag, only to see it come up 20 yards short of the pin. What are the first words you want to say? If they are, 'Oh, bad luck', then you really are a sport, but most people, I think, would love to say, as they rummage in their own bag, 'What club did you hit?' Please don't say these words. It's a loss-of-hole penalty in match play or a two shot penalty in stroke play.

However, if the person who hit the shot is your partner in an event, then by all means go ahead and ask him what club he hit. What advice you are allowed to give concerns the position of bunkers or hazards. You may, for example, have invited your friend to your golf club for the first time. As he's standing on the 4th preparing to hit a 'blind' tee shot, it is as well to inform him that in fact if he goes with the driver in his hands and strikes it well, then he'll be in the ditch that runs across the fairway over the other side of the hill. Either that, or he won't be your friend any longer.

Left: After missing a putt, you are quite entitled to try it again to see what went wrong. The best place to practise, however, is before you go out, on the practice putting green. That way you will miss less of the putts that matter.

It is customary for the player with the lowest handicap to drive off first from the first tee.

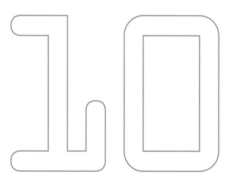

Rule 10

Order of Play: When standing on the first tee with your playing partners, there are a number of ways to determine who plays first. Customarily, the player with the lowest handicap will get the game under way, although you can toss a coin in the air or anything similar that appeals. When you have all reached your tee shots, the player who lies the furthest from the hole plays first and then the second furthest and so on. This continues until the hole is played out. The player who records the lowest number of strokes on that hole will play first, or 'have the honour' as it is termed, on the next tee.

If you drive the ball out of bounds, then you play another ball from the tee after your playing partners have driven off.

Don't worry if you accidentally play out of turn. There is no penalty. You're likely to get showered with abuse, however, from your playing partner if you tee off before him when you're not entitled. At least that's my experience.

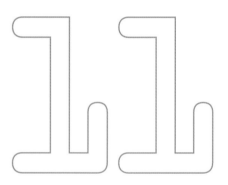

Rule 11

Teeing Ground: You're feeling very nervous as you stand on the first tee in a game with two people with whom you haven't played before. You go to address your ball and knock it off its tee. 'One,' says one of your amusing partners.

Don't be alarmed: it's a joke. You're allowed to tee it up again without penalty. Only if you were making a swing at the ball and you knocked it three inches off the tee would it count as one. Then you've every reason to feel alarmed. Embarrassed even.

Every club has what is known as the designated tees for that day. There will probably be at least three different tee markers: say, White for competitions, yellow for normal play, red for women. The idea is to tee off within two club lengths behind the tee markers. Most people, of course, tee off in a line with the markers because you don't want to give the course a yard more than you have to. The ball must be placed within the tee markers although you're allowed to stand outside them if you want.

The teeing ground on each hole will invariably feature at least three different tees: one for competition play; the tee of the day; and the ladies tee.

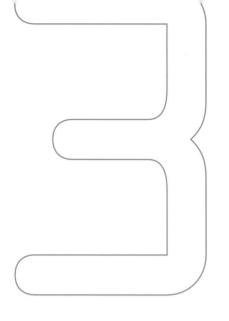

Rule 13

Ball Played as it Lies: From the moment your ball leaves the tee to when you reach the putting green, you must play it from where it lies. An exception is made during the winter months, from November 1 to March 30, when you will be able to improve your lie on the fairway, or follow a local rule if one is in operation. If your ball is in the trees you must not break any branches in an effort to get a decent swing at it. The only things you are allowed to move are loose objects, such as acorns or broken twigs, but only if they don't result in your moving the ball.

When in a bunker, you are not allowed to ground the club behind the ball. You are not allowed to smooth down the sand until after you've played your shot and if your ball has landed in a footprint, then sadly that's just tough luck. You are not allowed either to move any loose impediments such as leaves, but you are allowed to move stones if there is a real danger of your striking one on your downswing.

Remember that you are not allowed to ground your club before you play a shot from a bunker.

Always take care to repair any pitch-marks caused through your ball landing on the green.

Rules 16 and 17

The putting green: A ball on the putting green may be lifted and cleaned without penalty. A ball marker or a small coin is best for this job, but anything is allowed as long as you replace the ball precisely in the spot from where you picked it up. One inch to the side is not precise enough.

You can sweep away any loose impediments that lie between your ball and the hole. You may repair any pitchmarks left by inconsiderate people in front. You are not allowed to tap down any spike marks that stand on your route to the hole, however.

If you stand a long way from the hole you may either have the flag out or attended by a playing partner, who will remove it before your ball reaches the hole. You are not allowed to have the flag left in unattended. Well you are, but if your ball happens to go in the hole or strikes the flagstick then that's a two stroke penalty. If you are having the flag out make sure it is placed off the green or at least in a place where there is no chance of your striking it with your putt.

That would also be a two stroke penalty.

Below: The 18th at The Belfry, and perhaps the most famous water hazard in the world. The player drives from the left of the picture, over the first expanse of water, and then, from the fairway on the right, plays a second shot over the water again to the green.

Right: In the 1989 Ryder Cup at the Belfry, Payne Stewart elected to play from the hazard and if you look closely you can see he got the ball out. The trouble is it took him three shots to do it.

Rule 26

Water Hazards: A water hazard is any sea, lake, pond, river, ditch, or other open water course – whether containing water or not – and should be defined by yellow stakes. A lateral water hazard is one where it is deemed impracticable to drop the ball behind the said hazard, and should be defined by red stakes.

If your ball goes into a water hazard, you drop another ball under penalty of one stroke behind the hazard at the point of entry. What if you're not sure it went into the hazard? The rules say there must be reasonable evidence, or else you have to treat it as a lost ball. If you lose a ball, it means you have to go back and replay the shot from the original spot under penalty of one stroke. If your ball is lost in a lateral water hazard you must play another under penalty of one stroke within two clubs lengths of the point where the ball entered the hazard. If this is not possible, you can replay your shot from the original position, again adding a one shot penalty.

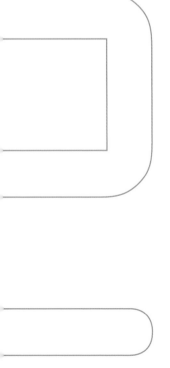

Rule 27

Ball Lost or Out of bounds: You're allowed to search for five minutes for a ball. If you can't find it within that time, you have to declare it lost and go back and play another from the spot where you hit it under penalty of one stroke. If you drive from the tee into a jungle and there's little chance of finding it, you are allowed to play a provisional ball to save time, but you're not allowed to play a second shot with that ball until the original has been declared lost. A ball is out of bounds if it lies wholly beyond any boundary fence or other area usually determined by white stakes. Under penalty of one stroke you play another from the original spot.

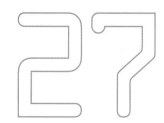

After driving into the heavy rough always make sure the ball you find is yours. In the 1994 Open, Faldo lost two shots after playing the wrong ball.

Rule 28

Ball Unplayable: You may declare your ball unplayable at any point on the course except when it is in or touching a water hazard, see Rule 26. You have three options. Under penalty of one stroke you may either: drop the ball within two club lengths of where the ball lies, though not nearer the hole; drop the ball behind the point where it lay though keeping the trouble between yourself and the hole with no limit on how far back you can go; trudge back to the spot from where you put yourself in this mess and replay the shot.

Rules 29, 30, 31, 32

Forms of Play: These are dealt with in detail on pages 104–105.

Once you have declared your ball unplayable the procedure is to drop a new ball from shoulder height.

ETIQUETTE

What it is and why it is so important

First things first: etiquette is not some obscure French sport. Indeed, the etiquette of golf, its protocol, is among the essential things that every beginner should know before setting out on his or her first round. As you learn the rules of this game, some of the ways and means will appear illogical and some unnecessary, but etiquette is not among them. At the very least, it will save you hassle from just about every other player you meet. It may even save your life.

For a little knowledge in golf can be a very dangerous thing, and a club a lethal weapon in the hands of someone who is not aware that 'fore' is not a polite variation on another four-letter word, but the code that golfers use to indicate that a ball is heading in the direction of another player.

You should never play a shot when there is a chance of hitting the players in front, but on courses where fairways are adjacent to one another, you will occasionally – or perhaps frequently at first! – strike a shot sufficiently off-line that it may disturb the players who are on another hole, in which case shout 'fore' as loud as you can. Etiquette is all about the general courtesies that one golfer has to show to another to make the game enjoyable. Most instruction books rarely bother about etiquette, preferring to deal in outlandish claims as to how they can have you hitting 300 yard drives in a matter of days. But you'll know just how imperative it is from the moment that your first perfectly-struck drive – whether it flies 300 yards or not – finishes in the divot left by another. For a golfer, the only thing worse, perhaps, is to walk up to a greenside bunker, mentally prepared to play the shot, only to find the ball in someone else's foot-print. Similarly, a green full of pitchmarks is a sad sight.

You'll probably be already familiar with some aspects of etiquette, even if your only experience of the sport is watching Nick Faldo on television. Not speaking when your playing partner is in the process of hitting a shot, for example. Or not shuffling about on the tee, when someone is about to play. But the most common breach of etiquette is by players who take too long to play the game. I've dealt with slow play separately, because it really has become the curse of the sport. First, though, some helpful hints on etiquette which will make you a pleasure to play with!

The things you need to observe

The first player to tee off on any hole is the player who has the honour, which is gained by whoever completed the previous hole in the fewest number of strokes. If the scores were the same, the preceding hole is taken into consideration, and so on.

On the tee, always stand opposite to the player who is about to drive off. When you're playing your shot, make sure your partners are opposite you too. If they're behind you, or at right angles to you, there is, at worst, the danger that you may hit them with your club on the backswing, or at best, it can implant the notion in your head that you may hit them, which is the last thing you either should or want to be thinking about.

Always make sure the group in front are out of range. A very rough rule of thumb here is to play when they've completed their second shots, and have started walking. But in any case you'll quickly grasp how far you can hit the ball and don't play until they've gone beyond what would be the bounds of your best drive.

Right: Always smooth over your foot-prints after playing a bunker shot. On most courses you will find a rake beside each bunker designed for the task.

Below: Never leave your golf bag on the putting green. The surfaces are closely mown and easily damaged by a bag containing such weight.

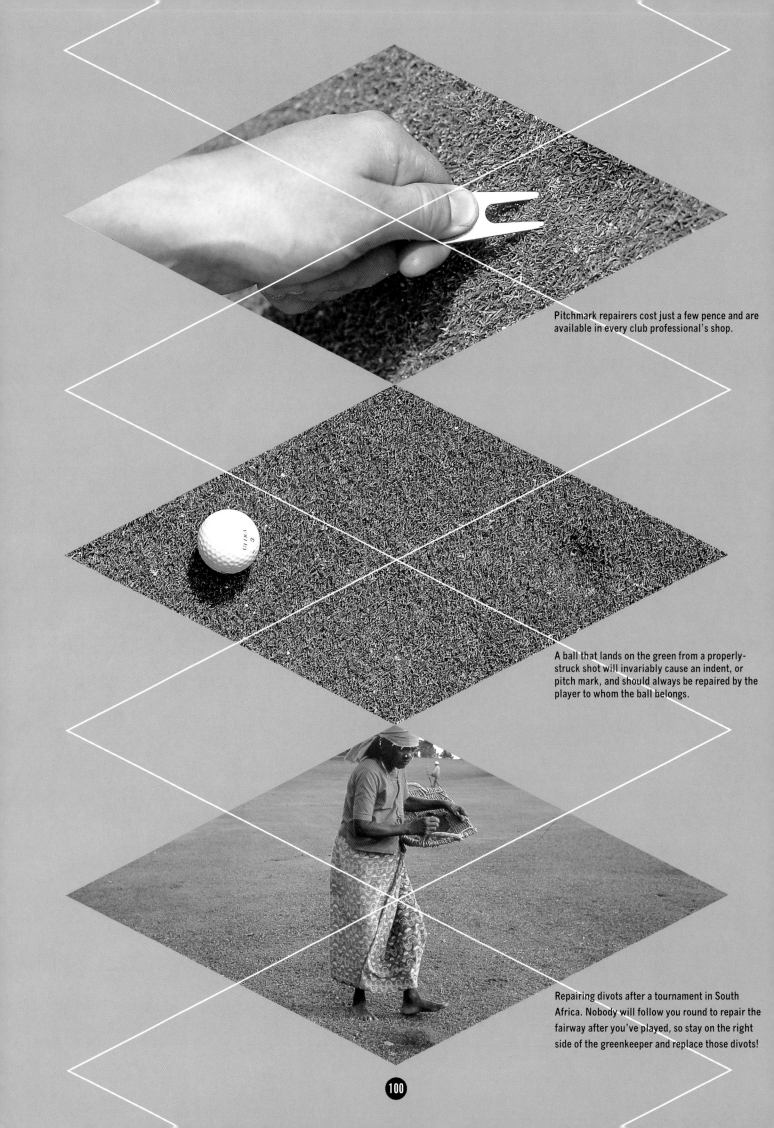

Pitchmark repairers cost just a few pence and are available in every club professional's shop.

A ball that lands on the green from a properly-struck shot will invariably cause an indent, or pitch mark, and should always be repaired by the player to whom the ball belongs.

Repairing divots after a tournament in South Africa. Nobody will follow you round to repair the fairway after you've played, so stay on the right side of the greenkeeper and replace those divots!

'A tolerable day, a tolerable green and a tolerable opponent supply - or ought to supply - all that any reasonably constituted human being should require in the way of entertainment.'

Lord Balfour

When taking a practice swing, it's as well not to take huge divots out of the tees unless you desire your name to appear on a 'Wanted' poster in the head green-keeper's hut. When in the trees or in a rough area of ground, always clear twigs, pebbles, conkers, or whatever, that you may hit either on your backswing or follow-through. These can be very dangerous both to yourself or someone else. The rules of golf do not allow you to move anything, however, that is still attached to its moorings, so don't get the machete out and start clearing branches that stand in your way or restrict your swing.

On any half-decent golf course, you'll notice a rake next to every bunker. Some golfers seem to think this is merely decoration but it is, of course, to smooth over any footprints, birdprints, dogprints and holes left trying to get the ball out.

Repairing a pitchmark is easy. If your ball has landed on the green from a distance away then it will almost certainly have left one. Pitchmark repairers are available from any professional's shop for a nominal sum.

Two 'never under any circumstances . . .' are pulling your trolley over any part of the green and leaving your bag on it while you putt. Whether carrying your own clubs or using a trolley, always leave them a few yards away from the edges of the green. In the winter, you may not be able to pull a trolley if a course is wet, but if you are, don't pull it through any water or within 10 yards of any green.

When on the greens, take care not to drag the spikes of your shoes across the putting surface. On well-kept greens this can leave an ugly scar. Spike marks are simply unavoidable on well-prepared surfaces. In big tournaments, you'll often hear professionals who are playing in the afternoon complain about the spike marks left by those who played their rounds in the morning. You can do your bit by treading carefully around the hole and generally not stomping around like an elephant. Leaning on your putter whilst on the green or when picking the ball out of the hole are also habits that are easy to lapse into but ones to avoid.

If one of your playing partners is putting from a long distance away, you could be asked to attend the flag. This involves holding it until the putt is on its way but then removing it before it reaches the hole. Take care that you don't damage the hole in the process of removal. The edges of the holes are easy to deface and, as you've only got an area four and a quarter inches in diameter to aim at in the first place, the last thing anyone wants is for that small target to be tampered with. This probably sounds like a hefty amount to remember before going on to the golf course, but a lot of it will simply slot into place from the moment you step on to the first tee.

Etiquette Do's and Don'ts

D O :

· Smooth over all footprints and holes left in a bunker.
· Repair not just your own pitchmark, but any others you see on a green.
· Take care not to damage the edge of the hole, either when removing the flagstick or your ball.

D O N ' T :

· Stand behind a player as he is about to tee off.
· Take lumps out of the tee with your practice swings.
· Ever leave your golf bag or trolley on a green.

101

'Why do I whistle all the time on the course?
It is to cut down on the boredom caused
by all this slow play on tour.'

Fuzzy Zoeller

A familiar scene for Langer followers.
The German studies the possibilities
before playing a shot...and studies....and
studies...and. . .

Klinsmann celebrates a goal for Germany.
Or perhaps it's his reaction to Langer
telling him: honest, I'll play more quickly
in future.

Slow play –
The curse of the game

One thing you'll quickly learn in golf is that no golfer ever admits to being slow. Calling a golfer slow is tantamount to questioning their parentage. When Severiano Ballesteros was once told at a tour event that he was being timed for slow play he went bananas, threatening to play in America rather than Europe.

Nick Faldo doesn't think he's slow. Bernhard Langer is the same. The subject has become one of the most sensitive in the sport. By my definition, the above three are all painfully slow, and, sad to say, it is because beginners tend to imitate the superstars, that many of the problems regarding slow play are now with us at every level of the sport.

Langer is a case in point. He'll place his tee peg in the ground, with the ball on it. He'll have at least a couple of practice swings. Then he'll move five yards behind the ball. He'll check for the wind strength. He'll come back to the ball. Another couple of looks to check for alignment. Klinsmann's probably scored a hat-trick before Langer has played a shot.

But at least the German has the perfect excuse. Every time he plays golf, every shot amounts to at least hundreds and often thousands of pounds. He can't afford a single mistake. He's not going out for an enjoyable afternoon's golf, he's going out to make a living.The trouble is, there are just too many golfers who are out for an afternoon's stroll who copy the whole tiresome routine. Cut it out! We've got to the stage now on some courses where to go round in four hours is considered an achievement. Last year, while on holiday, I was paired up with an American at 3.30pm and the professional told us we had to be in by 6.15pm. 'Should be able to get nine holes in then, shouldn't we?' the American said.

When we'd completed 18 with five minutes to spare, he looked at me as if I'd just forced him to do a marathon. But he was exhilarated too, and he confessed that it was the best that he had played for months. This is what happens when you just enjoy the game, and let it flow, and don't get bogged down by dogma.

I fear we have gone too far now for slow play to ever be eradicated and I'm sure once you're proficient at the game it will annoy you just as much as it does all who love the sport and can take or leave all the periphery.

But here are some basic tips that myself and my friends unconsciously abide by and why our fourball on a Friday afternoon never strays beyond three and a quarter hours.

If you're first or second to tee off, you should be ready, with club replaced in the bag, and bag over your shoulder or hand on trolley, ready to march off the moment your fourth player has completed his shot. This may sound a little unsociable to the last player but it isn't. Remember: you've got at least three hours to talk to them on the golf course, never mind how much time you spend afterwards in the clubhouse.

Again if you're first to tee off, don't delay everyone by marking your score for the previous hole. Do it while someone else is teeing off.

When playing your second shot, don't wait until your partner has played before sizing up the wind conditions, how far you've got to go, and what club to play. These are all things that can readily be done while they are playing. Be ready to hit your shot at the appropriate moment.

On the greens, there is no need to wait for your partner to have finished their putt before reading the line of your own. Of course, there are occasions when you are on the same line, and so you cannot without committing a gross breach of etiquette, but most times you'll find you can, without interrupting the thought processes of your colleague.

If all this sounds as though you're in a race, you'll discover that on the course it's a different matter. Golf, by its very nature, is a slow and time-consuming pursuit. What causes many of the problems is the people who abuse this basic fact, and it only takes a few golfers of this persuasion to clog up a course and so stretch out a round to five hours and sometimes even beyond for everyone.

Few people can concentrate for that length of time, and I promise you, the most enjoyable rounds of golf that you experience will be ones that take an hour less.

The other prime cause of slow play is an ignorance of the rules of golf. Some clubs have special rules, and the back of the scorecard will usually reveal these, but generally if you're playing with two or three other players, you should wave through any group of two players, or two-ball to give it the golfing term, who are playing behind. Thus you will help to keep the traffic moving. Additionally, if your group falls one clear hole behind the players in front, be it through looking for a lost ball or simply because you are less proficient at the game, then the match behind should be invited to pass.

Slow play can make golf the most boring game in the world, and the faces of Ernie Els and John Daly here are testimony.

SCORING

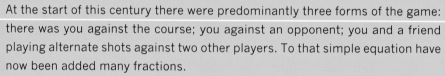

Foursomes, fourball, handicap etc

At the start of this century there were predominantly three forms of the game: there was you against the course; you against an opponent; you and a friend playing alternate shots against two other players. To that simple equation have now been added many fractions.

Medal play pits you against the course. It is simply a case of adding up how many shots you play on each hole and marking the figure down on a scorecard. Each hole has a par, or the amount of shots that it should be completed in by a professional or an amateur golfer who possesses a handicap of scratch (zero). If the par on each hole adds up to 72 after eighteen holes, then it follows that the player with a handicap of scratch has to shoot 72 to live up to his status. Few players get to be that good. In the beginning, you will be more than happy to average two shots above par for each hole. If you average that over three rounds which have been verified by a marker, you would be entitled to a handicap of 36 shots. As you become more proficient your handicap will obviously come down, one day, perhaps down to a single figure, a prized possession indeed.

Sadly, foursomes golf is rarely played these days, except at certain courses such as Brancaster in Norfolk. It is played in the Ryder Cup, however, where the Americans call it scotch foursomes. In foursomes, you and a partner play alternate shots. You hit all the drives either on the odd or even numbered holes. Fourballs golf is when you both play your own ball, and you pit your wits against two opponents doing the same. The best score on each hole by any player wins the hole for his team. That puts them one up. The winners are the pair who get so many holes ahead with one hole less to play. So, if a pair are four holes ahead with three holes to play, they are declared the winners four and three. It is the same in foursomes, although obviously each team only has one ball.

A game of singles match play uses the same format, only you are on your own. If you are playing someone off a lower handicap, then he will have to give you shots. You are allowed three-quarters of the difference, with halves rounded upwards. If, say, you are off 30 and your opponent 20 the difference is ten. Three-quarters of that sum is 7.5, so you will be entitled to eight shots. In foursomes golf, the number of shots given by one side is three-eights of the difference between each team's combined handicaps.

Where do you take these shots you're entitled to? You will notice on every scorecard a stroke index, in which each hole is graded in terms of difficulty

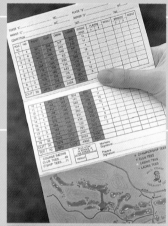

Virtually every scorecard lists the yardage for each hole, its par, stroke index, and has spaces for scores and stableford points.

Most players have a reputation for stroke or match play but Colin Montgomerie is adept at both.

from one to 18. If you are receiving five shots, you take them on the holes with a stroke index of one to five.

The great popularity of the game has inevitably spawned many more formats. There's greensomes, a variation on foursomes, where everybody drives off on every hole, you and your partner select your best drive, and then play alternate shots from thereon in. There's Texas Scramble, where a team of four selects their best drive, they all play their second shots from there, and then they select their best second shot etc, etc. As you can imagine scores in the 50's in this format are quite common even if you only get 1/10 of the combined handicaps in shots. There's also the shotgun start, where each team begins on a different hole, and so everyone finishes at roughly the same time.

One more that you should know about is the Stableford system. Most club golfers are unhappy with the medal strokeplay format because, although they receive their full handicap allowance, they know that one bad hole can wreck a good card. The more forgiving Stableford system allows for this by awarding points for every hole. If you get an eagle you get four points, a birdie three, a par two, a bogey one, and a double bogey or higher nothing at all. You're allowed 7/8ths of your handicap for this competition.

THE MAIN FORMS OF THE GAME

Game	Format	Handicap Allowance
Medal	Individual. Stroke play	Full
Stableford	Individual. Points	7/8ths
Foursomes	Team. Alternate shot m/play	3/8ths diff between teams
Fourballs	Team. Own ball m/play	3/4 diff between teams
Bogey	Individual. m/play	3/4

No players are better at foursomes and fourballs than Severiano Ballesteros and Jose-Maria Olazabal. Indeed they're so much in harmony they even walk in step.

Par, bogey, eagle etc

To the outsider it must often seem that golf has a language all of its own and consequently a conversation between two players in a bar must be bewildering. For example, 'You were putting for eagle on that hole, but you settled for a birdie. I once saw a man walk off with an albatross there, but I only got a par. Most times I settle for a bogey.' Er, excuse me but is this English we're talking here?

As early as the 1880's, a standard score in strokes was being assigned to holes on some courses in England. In 1890, in exasperation at the level of difficulty, Major Charles Wellman, playing at Great Yarmouth, is said to have exclaimed that the standard score of the course was a regular bogey man, referring to the music-hall song that was popular at the time, 'Hush, hush, here comes the bogey man'.

Bogey then became the score that a good amateur should complete for the course. This was always slightly more lenient than par, which became the standard for professionals. At many courses they were one and the same thing, but not always and for some professionals, scoring bogey became second-best, a recognition that they had failed to achieve par.

Over time, then, par became accepted as the score that a good player should achieve, not just over the course of a round but on each hole. If he slipped by one stroke at that hole he had a bogey. Drop two shots and it became a double bogey.

If a player achieves one under par at a hole it is a birdie, two under is an eagle and three under, a very rare occurrence, is accordingly an albatross.

A birdie dates back to 1899 and originates from the American slang word 'bird', which referred to anything wonderful. It was perhaps inevitable that other ornithological references would be used to describe golfing events that were still more sublime.

Top: Ornithological references in golf stem from the American slang word 'bird,' referring to anything marvellous. Three under par is a rare bird indeed: no wonder it's known as an albatross.

Bottom: Two under par on a hole is rare too and goes by the name of an eagle. In America three under par is often referred to as a double eagle, although what they look like heaven only knows.

'AB Smith tells the story from 1899: " . . . my ball . . . came to rest within six inches of the cup. I said 'that was one bird of a shot . . . I suggest that when one of us plays a hole in one under par he receives double compensation.' The other two agreed and we began right away, just as soon as the next one came, to call it a birdie."'

HB Martin, *Fifty Years of American Golf*, 1936

'Golf is a game based on honesty. Where else would someone admit to a seven on an easy par three?'

American professional Jimmy Demaret, 1956.

The end of a round, the end of our story. After the theory, it is time for the practice. And the very best of luck!

Glossary of golfing terms

A	Albatross	A score of three under par on a hole. In America it is referred to as a double-eagle.
B	Back-nine	The second set of nine holes on an 18 hole golf course. Sometimes referred to as the inward nine.
	Birdie	A score of one under par on a hole.
	Bogey	A score of one over par on a hole.
	Borrow	The amount a putt will deviate due to a slope of the green.
C	Carry	The distance from when a ball is struck to when it first lands.
	Chip	A low-running shot played from around the green to the putting surface.
D	Divot	A piece of turf removed when a shot is played.
	Dogleg	A hole that changes direction, either to the left or the right, halfway through its course.
E	Eagle	A score of two under par on a hole.
F	Fairway	The area of mown turf between tee and green.
	Fourball	A match between two teams of two players, each playing their own ball.
	Foursome	A match between two teams of two players, each playing one ball by alternate shots.
	Front nine	The opening nine holes on an 18 hole golf course. Sometimes referred to as the outward nine.
G	Green	An area of closely-mown grass prepared for putting.
H	Handicap	The system than enables players both to take on each other and the course on level terms. The worse a player is, the higher the handicap and the more shots he receives. If someone regularly goes around a course in 20 over par then they should have a handicap of 20 and will receive 20 shots towards their efforts of matching the par of the course.

Hook A mistimed shot that deviates severely to the left for the right-handed player.

L

Lie Situation in which a ball finishes after the playing of a stroke.

Long iron A description for those irons numbered 1-4

M

Matchplay Form of the game where holes won and lost are the determining factor rather than strokes played.

Mid-iron A description for those irons numbered 5-7

P

Par The standard score for each hole, and the entire course.

Pitch Lofted shot from around the green to the putting surface.

R

R&A The game's governing body, the Royal and Ancient Golf Club of St Andrews.

Rough The area of unmown grass that lies either side of the fairway.

S

Short iron A description for those irons numbered 8-9, the pitching wedge, sand wedge, and indeed any other wedges.

Shank Totally mistimed shot, usually with a short iron, where the ball comes off the junction between hosel and club-face and travels at right angles to the target intended.

Slice Mistimed shot where the ball deviates sharply to the right for the right-handed player.

Strokeplay Form of the game where the number of strokes played is the determining factor.

Sweet spot The precise spot in the middle of the club where the greatest possible mass can be delivered from the club face to the ball.

T

Tee Closely-mown area where the first stroke on a hole is played. The ball is generally played from a tee peg.

Y

Yips A nervous condition induced by poor chipping and putting which can render its victim totally unable to do either.

INDEX

Numbers in italics refer to illustrations